Stalked
THE HUMAN TARGET

First and foremost, this book is dedicated to the very brave men and women around the world who are victims of stalkers, bullying and targeting, some of whom have lost their lives. To all the incredibly courageous individuals who stepped forward to participate in this book. Thank you for bravely sharing your stories.

To Lionel Appelboom, thank you for your ongoing support and for being a dear and valued friend. You have been brave enough to help the most vulnerable people in our community – if there were more Lionel Appelbooms in the world, it would be a much safer place.

To the late Michael Campion, who was in my life for close to 30 years, always supporting and encouraging me. He faced many challenges with great strength and courage alongside his lovely wife and loving family.

To my dad, who passed away during the final stages of writing this book. I'm very grateful we had the chance to say what we needed to say to each other. I thank Uncle Russell and Aunty Raelene for making sure we had those very important moments.

Stalked
THE HUMAN TARGET

Stories of people pursued by stalkers and the
devastating effects on their lives

RACHEL CASSIDY

ROCKPOOL
PUBLISHING

A Rockpool book
PO Box 252
Summer Hill
NSW 2130
Australia
www.rockpoolpublishing.com.au
http://www.facebook.com/RockpoolPublishing

First published in 2018
Copyright Text © JD Leo Pty Ltd 2018
Copyright Design © Rockpool Publishing 2018

Design and typesetting by Jessica Le, Rockpool Publishing

ISBN 978-1-925682-49-6

Printed and bound in China
10 9 8 7 6 5 4 3 2 1

Disclaimer: This book contains the faithfully reported stories of victims of stalking to the best of their recollections. They contain the honestly held opinions of the victims or others. These are not necessarily the opinions of the author. Names and information have been changed to protect the victims and the perpetrators' identities. This book is not intended to provide professional counselling to victims or legal advice; if victims feel their life is in danger or they are emotionally distressed they should seek professional advice.

Contents

Foreword

Having spent over 25 years with Life Education Australia, including a decade as its chairman, I have been involved in many areas of the development of our curriculum especially in relation to the issues of bullying. Bullying experienced at an early age reflects itself in behaviours well beyond the initial bullying incidents, and the extension into stalking and family violence is common place in those whose behaviour is not addressed at an early age.

Storytelling is the most effective way of communicating these hard social problems and Rachel uses stories to provide the reader with an in-depth look at some real life experiences of the victims of stalking. Also addressing the current state of play in both the legal system and clinical treatment areas, Rachel adds some solutions to this tale of pain and suffering.

Writing from the heart as someone who has experienced firsthand the issues discussed, Rachel is well qualified to publish this enlightening work.

Paul Wheelton AM
Knight of St John, Wheelton Philanthropy,
Director of Life Education Australia Foundation

It's a very sad world when we need to have books written on bullying and stalking. I have known Rachel for over 20 years and have witnessed atrocious behaviour from a number of people, some of whom claimed to be her friends, who severely bullied her. Rachel appeared to 'take it on the chin' but deep down has been greatly affected. I believe these type of people are appalling bullies and should be ashamed of their actions. They are bullying people to make themselves look good and/or to advance their own status.

I applaud Rachel for having the courage to write this valuable book. I believe it should not only be made available to all victims of bullying and stalking it should be compulsory reading as a class text in schools. This would not only help victims but may stop, or at least slow down, the next generation of bullies and stalkers. If you are reading this book and you have been bullied, *you are not alone* (sadly).

Cr Tony Holland
Knox City Council, Victoria

Rachel provides us with a current and disturbing insight into just how far stalking has permeated into the lives of both known and regular Australians, including her own. Rachel also gives an insight into how to help all of us recognise the early signs of someone who presents as a friend, admirer or love interest, but due to an underlying mental disturbance can quite literally blow up your life – mentally, emotionally, physically and spiritually – as well as creating very real safety issues for yourself, family, friends and colleagues. Stalking is no longer the experience of public figures and Hollywood celebrities, it has unfortunately made its way into everyday society with some victims paying the ultimate price to a disturbed mind. Never feel the need to be endlessly 'nice' to someone who dotes on you to an extreme, yet disturbingly unwelcome, level. They may be harmless – but they may not be.

Claudia Keech OAM
Australian American Media

Preface

I decided to write this book in the hope that I can shine a light on the issues of bullying and stalking so that victims feel they have a voice and are not isolated, that they are not alone. I have been the target of a stalker's relentless pursuit and also endured traumatic episodes of being bullied. Celebrities are the highest profile victims of stalkers, but ordinary people like myself are also stalked, harassed and bullied. It is a frightening situation. I certainly acquired an understanding of the scale of the problem when I became embroiled in the stalker's world of madness. If I can help just one human target by writing this book, then I will feel that stepping forward to be a voice for victims has made some small difference.

I can relate to and feel empathy for many of the stories I heard repeated over and over by victims of domestic, school and workplace bullying and stalking – families being torn apart, careers being destroyed, credibility and reputations being left in tatters, wild and ridiculous stories that have no substance circulating, and friends, family, work colleagues, government agencies and the legal system being used and abused.

As psychologists and those working in the legal system explained to me, stalkers and bullies can gather many troops around them, often spreading outrageous and malicious stories with the kind of obsessive determination which is military in its planning. Followers can appear mesmerised by the often-charismatic façade that perpetrators can put on, and so unknowingly they can be manipulated into joining forces to support the stalker – no matter what the consequences, the more layered the situation becomes, the harder it is for those supporters to step back and look at the full picture with clear vision.

As forensic psychiatrist Michele Pathé explains in her book *Surviving Stalking*, the term 'stalking by proxy' is used when a stalker recruits a network of support people by giving them one-sided, skewed information about the target. This is exactly what happens to many victims, and it can create a wall of silence among the stalker's followers, spread a maze of untruths about the victim and obscure who the perpetrator really is. This makes it impossible for the target to defend themselves – because they don't know what is happening or what they are being accused of, it is impossible to fight the allegations or correct the misinformation. It's hard to confront an enemy when you can't identify who the enemy is.

With the development of computer technology has come a new wave of perpetrators. A member of parliament I spoke to used the phrase the 'keyboard terrorist'. Online bullying and stalking is exceptionally damaging to the victim. Electronic files can be opened or go missing, computers can be hacked into and mobile phones accessed, allowing emails and text messages that victims have not written appearing to be sent from their devices, and contacts databases can be infiltrated. The stalker can thus circulate a barrage of false information that impacts on the victim's credibility and reputation – there are many victims of this type of stalking, including Barbara (see page 65–77).

As lawyer Vic Rajah says, 'Malicious and insidious actions such as hacking into personal email accounts or gaining access to phone text messages and sending purported messages from the victim to third parties can violate the victim's sense of self. This can lead to the damaging of the victim's personal and professional relationships and affect their credibility and reputation. Such actions serve to enshrine the power of the perpetrator and are designed to destroy the will and support networks of the victim.

'With such a great focus on social media platforms, it is virtually impossible to distinguish between fact and fiction,' he says. 'A predator who adopts someone else's online persona can inflict irreparable harm. The most worrisome aspect is this can occur remotely via a computer. It can be very convincing when people see emails or letters they think you have written or when your personal information gets distorted. In the end, they don't know what to believe – and it's human nature to think that where there's smoke there's fire. But, of course, that's often not the case at all. I have learned that rumours can gather a life of their own. Smart, well-educated stalkers, particularly those who have a public profile or are high functioning, can claim that it is in the public interest to pursue an individual or publicise rumours and wild accusations.'

Vic Rajah also believes that the media should show greater accountability. 'Although there are many journalists who cover stories on stalking and bullying responsibly, at times, either wittingly or unwittingly, the media has played a role in aiding stalking or bullying behaviours by sensationalising a story – so the victim has to endure public scrutiny on top of being targeted by the perpetrator. The victim is pulled into a situation where they have to mount a defence when in fact they are innocent. The public exposure also leaves the victim vulnerable to other possible bullying or targeting episodes, as other perpetrators can sweep in, sensing the victim may not be believed and has lost a certain amount of credibility and reputation.'

Some stalkers go to great lengths to profile their victims – getting close to them, gathering personal information and watching the way they react to certain situations. Depending on the stalker's state of mind, at times they can claim similarities between their life and the victim's, saying they had the same experiences, or they frequent the places that are the victim's usual haunts. The stalker can become totally obsessed.

When I was stalked, it wasn't the first time I had been targeted. I was bullied at primary school. I had feet that turned inwards (which no longer turn inwards these days, so I can happily wear high heels) so in my early years I was clumsy and struggled. Children can be cruel and because I was different from other kids – and I was shy and small framed with curly, frizzy hair that never stayed in place and freckles – I endured continuous taunting, so I spent many agonising days trying to avoid kids throwing sticks, calling me names or pushing me over, which was easy to do with my built-up support shoes and unsteady feet. The vulnerability I felt then is something that people who prey on others can sense and that they can capitalise on.

Like many victims, initially I blamed myself. But I know that I didn't do anything to trigger the stalker or ignite the bullies. Through speaking to so many victims of bullying and stalking, and to the experts who study those behaviours, I know that the perpetrators often have narcissistic personalities, false senses of reality and entitlement, or other mental health issues – and if it wasn't one particular human target, someone else would be the object of their obsession. Now I don't think about what I could have done to stop the stalker or the bullies, as once you are their focal point then you become their target. In my case the threat to me physically and psychologically went on for long periods of time, which exasperated my ability to extract myself and get on with my life. I'm now focused on helping other victims recognise the early signs and the behaviour to hopefully give them a chance to escape the trauma I was once subjected to.

Since my own experiences, I have educated myself about the subject and have gained a greater level of understanding of stalking behaviour. I am not afraid of the stalker any more or of the bullies – I refuse to give them any power. And I have an incredible network of supporters who are committed to ensuring I never suffer in this manner again. But it took me years to find this understanding and these support systems. Now I am strong enough to be able to be a voice for other victims.

I remain deeply disturbed by the very notion of what stalkers and bullies are capable of doing, and the feelings of helplessness, isolation and utter despair felt by victims. There are so many others out there, like me and dance teacher Mark Wilson (who nowadays has a wall of protection from any possible stalking situation), who have been targeted by stalkers and bullies. In the course of writing this book, I spoke to many people who have been targeted by a stalker or been bullied. They come from all walks of life and from very diverse circumstances, and each has a unique story. I could feel their pain and see the terror in their eyes as, one after another, they recalled their own terrifying experiences with the one human being who targeted them and tried to destroy their world. They called the person a 'bully', 'criminal', 'perpetrator', 'stalker' – names that hang in the air but don't begin to convey the horrors that were inflicted on them, which include the threats of physical attacks and acts of violence.

Victims need to tell their stories – if they feel comfortable doing so – so that more people in our communities are aware of the dangers, the signs, that someone is being targeted, and so those who are affected know they are not alone. If you have a physical injury, you can seek medical attention – the damage is visible and people will try to assist. When you are being targeted and psychologically abused, there are no physical scars. So many victims feel isolated and suffer alone. This is compounded by the fact that they often attempt to protect their family and friends from becoming embroiled in the stalking. If they do ask for support or try to explain what is happening, those around them often become confused and misjudge the situation – others often find it hard to comprehend the level of damage being caused to the victim. Of course, some victims of stalking and bullying behaviours also have physical injuries and, in the most extreme cases, have sadly lost their lives.

During the times I was bullied and stalked, some onlookers became involved, siding with the perpetrators and thus helping to create a lynch mob that escalated the perpetrator's corrosive power. Thankfully, a few people – not many – refused to be influenced by the crowd, spoke up for me and gave me great support. I will always remember their help with great affection and gratitude. They did the right thing – and that's what I would urge anyone who witnesses others being stalked or bullied to do. If you see anyone being targeted as I was, if you hear stories that are uncharacteristic of a person you know, like the ones told about me, take the time to find out what is really happening. Give the victim your understanding and also be outspoken in support of them. This is not the time to remain silent or to join the tribe, but a time to take a stand and stamp out bullying behaviour.

During and after the episodes of being stalked and bullied, I suffered health issues that I had not previously had, including nose bleeds, stomach cramps, skin rashes, sleep deprivation and absolute extreme exhaustion. I was hospitalised several times and, after having high blood pressure that would settle then rise again when I was being targeted, I now have damage to the left side of my heart – the bullies literally broke my heart emotionally and then physically. I lost a considerable amount of weight and looked gaunt. When I lost my hair through the trauma, I was diagnosed with alopecia, which required regular painful treatments of cortisone injections straight into my scalp to try to regain my hair. I started researching where to acquire natural-looking hair pieces and eventually a wig.

It was debilitating being relentlessly targeted and persecuted and at the same time trying to regain my health and rebuild my life. But slowly, step by step, I did it and rebuilt my life surrounded by loving friends and family with a peace and happiness that I could once only dream would be achievable in my life again. Today my hair has grown back, I manage my fragile heart and I have an abundance of energy. So now I am strong enough to help others, which gives me some meaning to the relentless targeting and horrendous circumstances I once found myself subjected to.

I have no intention of discussing my personal story publicly. This book is not about me and I don't want my story to overshadow those of the other victims. My intention is to provide the community with a greater understanding of bullying and stalking behaviours through extensive interviews and research and to give a voice to the victims who want to tell their stories to help others.

If a stalker or any other bully ever entered my life again, I am now ready and equipped and know my legal rights through the knowledge I have acquired. The stalker and the bullies will never get close enough to me again to cause the utter devastation they did previously – even though I have no doubt some would use any reason to justify their behaviour and consider activating any channels to re-engage with me and once again fuel their obsession. But I am no longer prepared to be anyone's human target or to engage with bullies. And, with the support, kindness and encouragement of the many incredibly compassionate people I have around me, I will continue my crusade to help as many vulnerable people as I can.

I am now enjoying my life as a human being, not as a human target.

Being the victim of a stalker, as lawyer Vic Rajah says, makes you 'feel absolutely set upon by another individual and quite often the person doing the stalking is thinking that by using the legal process, turning up the heat through government bodies, manipulating the media or the system, they can achieve their objectives. Sometimes the stalker can be psychotic. Alternatively, a stalker may have a political or a non-psychotic motive which is quite irrational and very devious. But the effects on the individuals who are subjected to these types of episodes are similar – they are put under stifling, irrational, crazy pressure.'

As the number of people – and sometimes organisations and the media – doing the stalker's bidding increases, Vic Rajah says: 'It can be absolutely terrifying for victims because there are new bullies to contend with and more insinuations flying around. A high-functioning perpetrator can hide behind a veil of sanity and go about their life in a seemingly normal way, all the time hiding certain aspects of their life. Under normal conditions, the perpetrator would be challenged, with the community concluding that the stories they are telling are total nonsense. But, with repetition, the court of public opinion will often blame the victim. The perpetrator can make a decent person feel completely and utterly boxed into a corner because they are in the clutches of a very sophisticated stalker, bully or extortionist.'

Psychologist Gary Rubin, who specialises in bullying issues, believes the incidence of stalking and bullying is increasing. 'Over the last ten years I have seen a significant increase in clients who have presented with severe trauma associated with being exposed to bullying and stalking,' he says. 'I believe this can be attributed to the heightened capacity for exposure through social media and the like. People with low self-esteem or people with certain personality characteristics or personality disorders – often undiagnosed – such as narcissistic personality disorder and borderline personality disorder are more likely to engage in these types of behaviours.

'The difficulty in trying to manage or negotiate with someone with these characteristics is that they often take no responsibility for their behaviour and more often than not truly believe that their actions are reasonable. Their need for power and control – and sometimes the addition of an attachment or jealousy issue – often overpowers any consequential thinking and hence the victim can be exposed to some relentless abuse.'

Unfortunately, the corporate sector, indeed the general working environment, is ripe for fostering these type of bullying, stalking or abusive relationships. Status, hierarchy and group dynamics are all heightened in the workplace, just as they are in the school grounds. The stalkers and bullies are often attracted to those with certain personality types, and vice versa, and therefore 'it is not uncommon for victims of this trauma to have repeat experiences'. Gary Rubin recommends that victims seek counselling, which, he believes, assists them not only in managing the trauma while it is occurring but also to understand how to prevent repeating certain patterns from occurring again.

As Associate Professor Debra Bateman says, 'Every person has the right to feel safe in every aspect of their world. A challenge to a person's safety inhibits their ability to fully participate in their own life. Supporting those who face any form of harassment, bullying or stalking begins with hearing their stories, which offer an important and educative insight, as well as a provocation for our community. The impetus for our society is how we respond, in looking after our victims who suffer in silence and moreover how we manage those for whom personal and public boundaries have no meaning.'

***

I have been very fortunate in the course of writing about stalking and bullying behaviours to have received a great deal of support from experts in the field, who have been extremely generous in sharing their research and experiences. I would like to express my gratitude to them all, and most particularly to the following:

Troy McEwan is an associate professor in clinical and forensic psychology at the Centre for Forensic Behavioural Science in Melbourne, Australia, and senior psychologist at the Victorian Institute of Forensic Mental Health. Her research expertise is in the field of forensic psychology, with a specific focus on complex criminal behaviours, including stalking, family violence, sexually harmful behaviour, threats and arson. She is the author of more than 50 books, book chapters and research articles on these topics, including co-author of the Stalking Risk Profile, a risk assessment instrument for stalking that is used around the world. In addition to her ongoing clinical work, Troy has undertaken research funded by the Australian Research Council into the assessment and treatment of stalkers, and regularly provides training about stalking to clinicians, police and others who work with stalkers and their victims.

Dr Lorraine Sheridan, an internationally renowned forensic psychologist, lectures at Curtin University in Perth, Western Australia. She is a police-accredited offender profiler and compiles psychological reports related to offenders, highlighting the risks posed by known or unknown suspects. She regularly gives case management advice to the police, security personnel, celebrities and ordinary people on stalking, harassment, violence, risk assessment, malicious communications and similar topics.

Vic Rajah is a Melbourne-based lawyer who specialises in family law and acts for victims of domestic violence, bullying and stalking. He was awarded a Centenary of Federation medal for his community work on youth issues and currently is the deputy chair of a not-for-profit organisation that provides child intervention, education and support services.

Gary Rubin, who has more than a decade of experience as a psychologist, works with individuals, couples and families from all backgrounds. He uses a variety of approaches that he believes will be most effective, based on both the issue the client presents with and the experience he has in understanding what will best suit the person he is assisting. Gary believes that the issues presented in counselling are often symptoms of the underlying issues, and hence 'deeper' as opposed to 'band-aid' therapy will provide positive and sustainable change. Gary has extensive experience with clients presenting with significant mental health issues associated with traumas such as bullying and stalking.

Peter Ryan, former deputy premier of the state of Victoria, minister for police and member for Gippsland South, practised law for almost 20 years, specialising in litigation and handled bullying, victimisation and stalking cases.

Except where a full name is given, names of perpetrators and victims, together with their friends and colleagues, have all been changed to protect their identities.

Introduction

When I began writing this book, I set up media alerts with key words to capture all types of stalking incidents and news stories from across the globe. The alerts were coming in daily and it wasn't long before they were taking over my inbox – there were reams of reports, research papers and blogs. I spent hours trawling through report after report in disbelief about the prevalence of stalking all around the world. I started to realise that this was an epidemic.

To an outsider, the stalker's actions may appear to be minor indiscretions, but the constant unwanted attention, relentless harassment and utter terror of being a human target can have chilling cumulative effects. Some stalkers can't stop calling or texting their victims while others stalk via the internet. Some leave threatening notes on cars, follow their victims, watch their homes, take their mail and in some cases physically attack them. Stalking is very prevalent – it has been experienced by a shockingly high proportion of the population – and in some cases has dire consequences, including the suicide or murder of victims. According to the Australian Bureau of Statistics, one in five adult women (1.6 million) and one in 13 men (663,800) have experienced stalking in their lifetime. These are indeed alarmingly high statistics.

In 2001 while he was researching his book *I'll Be Watching You*, Richard Gallagher says that, 'I interviewed many victims and, despite the huge diversity of background, profession, domestic situation etc, I was impressed – frequently overwhelmed – by what they all had in common: their courage and their determination to carry on with their lives. Frequently, they had used the most appalling circumstances as a springboard into a new, even more productive life than they had led before their ordeal. An example of this was one lady who had been stalked for many, many years. She had, at the time I met her, become a figurehead for stalking victims. "Did she have any regrets?" I asked – rather crassly – "No!" She said she would have been a shy, submissive wife and not the person who could address a huge conference, change the British law and be the first person the TV called upon. That would never have happened without her stalker: he tried to destroy her. He failed in that because he made her great and I salute her.'

'When a high-profile celebrity is allegedly being stalked, the media at times can manufacture provocative headlines, promoting and escalating the drama, even though some of those very same news outlets are relentlessly pursuing the very same singers, actors and politicians,' says lawyer Vic Rajah. Lawyer and former MP Peter Ryan says: 'I think the media in a contemporary world tends to shape opinion rather than report opinion and I think the general nature of the media in the age in which we live is such that there is enormous competition in the marketplace, very particularly online, in all its different forms. There is a need for spontaneous responses and dynamic headlines and angles.' With stalking, 'the media tends to jump to a position very quickly and these days it's often difficult to do a truly analytical piece, which deals with a particular matter of current interest in any great depth,' he says. As a result, 'the media plays a very significant part'.

It is certainly true that celebrities are at increased risk of being hounded by stalkers. There are many reported high-profile examples of alleged stalkers. News reports state singer Beyonce had to increase security at one of her shows in fear of a British stalker, who was sending her threatening letters, labelling her an imposter and claiming he was attempting to help the singer; the stalker was issued with an anti-harassment order in 2011. Former Miss Universe Jennifer Hawkins filed an apprehended violence order against a stalker, who was ordered to stay at least 100 metres away from her and forbidden to assault, threaten, harass or intimidate her.

Hugh Jackman had a crazed fan throw an electric razor full of her own pubic hair at him in a New York gym. The woman, who was arrested after this stunt, had previously been spotted at the actor's home and at his daughter's school. It's been reported that David Letterman has been the centre of obsessions more than once – including one woman committing suicide after a long-term obsession. The man who stalked Madonna threatened to cut her from 'ear to ear' if she did not marry him. Rihanna obtained a restraining order against a fan who broke into her neighbour's house, believing it was hers, slept in what he thought was her bed and stole items from the house. In 2012 actress Mila Kunis was awarded a three-year restraining order against a stalker who had been busted once for breaking into her home, then caught outside a Los Angeles gym she was attending. Michael Douglas and Catherine Zeta-Jones. Justin Bieber. Conan O'Brien. Halle Berry. Justin Timberlake. Jewel. The list goes on and on and on.

In extreme cases, stalkers have resorted to killing their victims.

The killing of John Lennon outside his New York apartment building in December 1980 by Mark Chapman was the moment when celebrity stalking first rose to public prominence. In March the following year US President Ronald Reagan was shot and injured by John Hinckley, who was trying to impress actress Jodie Foster. Hinckley had sent love letters and poems to Foster, who had played a teenage prostitute in the 1976 Martin Scorsese film *Taxi Driver*.

California passed the first anti-stalking law in 1990 after the murder of Rebecca Schaeffer, the star of television show *My Sister Sam*, Schaeffer was shot by Robert Bardo, who had a long history of stalking young celebrities. In July 1989 he used a private investigator to locate her home address, then showed up at her apartment. After a short conversation Schaeffer asked him not to come back to her home but he showed up a second time and shot her in the chest. She was pronounced dead at Cedars-Sinai Medical Centre.

But stalking can happen to anyone. It happened to me.

Stalking targets are not only high-profile celebrities. They come from all walks of life. They can be male as well as female.

As Associate Professor Troy McEwan explains in chapter 1 (see page 10), stalking has proved difficult to effectively legislate against because of the range of connotations the term *stalking* has come to be imbued with. Indeed, stalking as a crime is an inherently difficult concept to define because it often involves not one but a range of behaviours – and on the surface these behaviours may appear to be normal. For example, phoning or sending text messages is normal behaviour, but not when you receive 50 or 60 a day, as some of the targets I spoke to did, and/or they are of a threatening or malicious nature. The range of behaviours that are typical of stalkers can include:

- numerous phone calls, text messaging, voice messaging
- threatening or obscene calls and messages
- sending letters, notes, faxes, emails, 'gifts' or other unwanted material
- cyberstalking, including assuming the target's or another's identity
- following, lying in wait for the target
- maintaining surveillance or spying
- trespassing
- interfering with or vandalising property
- ordering or cancelling goods and services on the target's behalf
- spreading malicious gossip
- destroying the target's personal and professional reputations
- starting false legal actions against the target
- recruiting third parties to help
- making direct or indirect threats
- direct physical approaches, which may result in harm
- targeting and/or harming family members, lovers,

friends, work colleagues
- harming the target's pets
- threatening suicide.

Criminalisation is beneficial in placing curbs on stalkers although, because of the nature of the crime, its effects are limited. And it certainly can never fully repair the shattered lives of the targets who have been preyed upon and live with the terror and devastation wracked by the people who harass and persecute others with unwanted and obsessive attention.

Part I

Chapter 1

What is Stalking?

For more than 13 years Associate Professor Troy McEwan has worked with people who stalk, 'originally as part of my doctoral research and then subsequently as both an assessing and treating psychologist, and as a researcher.' For her doctorate, she 'was supervised by Professor Paul Mullen, who was one of the first people in the world to undertake research into stalking in the 1990s,' she explains. 'I chose to continue my involvement with both research and practice in the area of stalking for a few different reasons. A close colleague asked me to co-write a manual for assessing stalkers immediately after the conclusion of my doctoral thesis. That led to continued research and to my ongoing clinical specialisation in this area.

'Understanding why someone chooses to act in this way, and to continue to act in this way in spite of all opposition, is fascinating to me, both as a clinician and a researcher,' Troy McEwan says. In this chapter, she defines the breadth of behaviours that make up stalking and its prevalence, looks at types of stalkers, why they do it and how victims are affected.

Stalking defined

Stalking is a constellation of behaviours by one person that targets another. The contact or communication with the target is unwanted and repeated, and causes some level of distress, fear and/or harm. It is defined by its repetitive pattern – one-off unwanted behaviour does not constitute stalking. A range of behaviours might be part of a pattern of stalking, from otherwise-innocuous actions such as emailing, leaving gifts or visiting the target at home or work, through to actions that would be crimes in themselves, such as threatening or physically assaulting someone. The most commonly reported stalking behaviours are unwanted telephone calls, emails and physical approaches to the target. In fact, the behaviours that make up stalking are really only limited by the stalker's imagination, which can mean that it can be very difficult for the target of the stalking to get people to believe the very odd things that the stalker is doing.

As a recognised behaviour, stalking is a relatively new phenomenon. It was only defined as a problem in the 1980s, after a number of high-profile cases that led to very serious or even fatal violence. It has been a crime in almost all English-speaking jurisdictions since the 1990s. This recognition that stalking could be seen as a crime was preceded by significant social changes that included the increased awareness of and prosecution of violence against women and domestic violence, both of which have relevance to stalking. There was also an increasing intolerance towards and fear of violence, along with increasing fear of crime more generally in the wake of the emergence of 'tough-on-crime' politics.

Classifying stalkers' behaviours

Stalking can occur in many different situations and relationships. Because of how varied stalking can be, a lot of different systems have been developed to classify stalking so it can be more easily understood. One typology that is widely used to classify stalkers and their behaviours was developed in the 1990s by Paul Mullen, Michele Pathé and Rosemary Purcell, based on their work with the perpetrators and victims. This is useful in practice because the different types are associated with different outcomes and ways of managing the behaviour.

This classification system describes three characteristics of stalking; this combination of characteristics produces five stalker 'types'. The three aspects are: the nature of the prior relationship between stalker and target; the apparent initial motivation for contact between the stalker and target, and the presence and nature of any mental illness of the stalker. The classifications are not perfect or mutually exclusive, and some cases do not fit any of the identified types. But these types do help to build an understanding of a case and can guide the kinds of questions that should be asked of the stalker and the victim.

The first type is the *rejected stalker*. This group begins to stalk after the breakdown of a close relationship, usually an intimate sexual relationship (however brief), but it can also emerge from the breakdown of a familial relationship, a close friendship or even a long-standing therapeutic relationship with a counsellor. The stalking is motivated by a desire to resume the relationship, take revenge for its end or, commonly, a combination of both. It is unusual for stalkers in this group to experience severe mental illnesses, although often depression and substance misuse is observed around the time of the stalking as the person struggles to cope with the loss of the relationship. The rejected stalker may have an underlying personality disorder.

The *resentful stalker* type is somewhat different in that they target strangers or acquaintances whom they perceive to have mistreated them in some way (or because they represent an organisation that has provoked their wrath). The stalking is motivated by a desire to right the perceived wrong. These stalkers are often very self-righteous and feel justified in their actions. Over time the stalking becomes a way of regaining a sense of power and control. Often these stalkers present with personality disorders or severe mental illness with paranoid delusions.

The *incompetent suitor stalker* wants an intimate relationship but lacks the social skills and/or desirability to establish one successfully. This group targets strangers or acquaintances whom they find attractive and the stalking usually commences in a gauche attempt to get a date. They can become angry and aggressive if their attempts are rebuffed, but they persist in spite of all attempts to dissuade them in the belief that they will eventually succeed. Some in this group are extremely egocentric and do not understand why someone would refuse their advances. Many do not suffer from any mental disorder, but disorders that impact on social skills, such as autism spectrum and developmental disorders, are not uncommon.

The *intimacy-seeking stalker* is in pursuit of a relationship too, and also targets strangers and acquaintances. However, their pursuit is marked by intense feelings of love for the target and they seek love in return. Often such feelings are driven by the symptoms of a mental illness characterised by delusions about the target (who, for example, they may believe is their husband or wife). In some cases the stalker is just intensely infatuated and believes that the longed-for love will eventuate if only they persist. Severe personality disorders are not uncommon in this group.

The *predatory stalker* targets strangers, or less frequently acquaintances, with the goal of achieving some sort of sexual gratification. The stalking forms part of a wider array of sexually deviant behaviours and usually takes the form of spying, following, loitering and sometimes sexual assault. This group differs from the incompetent and intimacy seeking because they do not want a relationship with the victim – they simply want sex or sexual gratification. The most common diagnoses in this group are sexual disorders, depression and substance misuse.

Who are stalkers?

Most people have the potential to engage in stalking, although some are more susceptible than others. Stalking is a behaviour, and like any other behaviour, people will do it if they think it will achieve an important goal. People who stalk almost always do so in response to a highly emotional situation which, they believe, involves the target. The emotions associated with the situation might be negative – for example, anger, frustration, feelings of betrayal or hurt – or they might be positive, like hope, lust and happiness. The common characteristic is that the emotions are very strong and so demand a response from the target to change them in some way. The related behaviours are generally directed towards the victim because the situation that has triggered the emotions is linked to that person. Depending on whether the target responds in the way intended or desired, the stalker might then feel the need to continue to try to influence them.

In the context of all of that, the stalker gets very focused on their own emotions and desires and that often means that they don't pay attention to the target's thoughts or feelings. It's important to recognise that many people who stalk would not think of their behaviour as stalking (which of course does not mean that it isn't). As Troy McEwan notes, most people who stalk tend to focus on each behaviour individually without seeing the impact of the pattern of behaviour on the victim. So for them it is 'just a phone call' and then 'just a few text messages', whereas for the target it is a barrage of attempted contacts. Of course, there are also cases where the stalker is well aware of the impact of their actions. When the stalking is motivated by a sense of mistreatment and feelings of anger, there is also often a sense that the stalker thinks the victim deserves to feel as bad as they do, so they keep targeting them in a never-ending attempt to get even.

Overall, more men stalk than women, and they do tend to stalk in slightly different contexts. More men stalk after a relationship has broken down – research finds they account for about 80 per cent of this kind of stalking. A smaller proportion of female stalkers target ex-partners; in some research undertaken in Australia and Sweden, about 60 per cent of male stalkers were targeting an ex-partner compared with about 40 per cent of the female stalkers. Women were more likely to target a neighbour, a former friend or family member, or a professional contact (such as their doctor or lawyer).

If you remove the ex-partner stalkers from the equation, there are still more male stalkers overall, but the ratio of men to women becomes more even. You also get a lot more stalkers who are targeting victims of the same gender, including a significant proportion of women stalking women (50 per cent of female stalkers in the research compared with 13 per cent of men who targeted men).

However, while there are differences in overall patterns of stalking between men and women, there doesn't seem to be much difference in the kinds of behaviours used by stalkers of either gender. There has been a reasonable amount of research looking at violence by female stalkers, and that suggests that rates of physical violence are much the same, regardless of whether the stalker is male or female. Women also seem to be equally threatening and cause as much property damage. The only thing that does seem to be slightly different between male and female stalkers is that the women stalkers are more often diagnosed with mental illness or personality disorder. However, that might just reflect the fact that women are more often diagnosed with these things in the general population, rather than being something specific to female stalkers. Also, rates and information vary according to where the sample is drawn from.

Psychologist Gary Rubin explains that, in his opinion, 'there is some evidence that females having conflict with other females in the workplace outweighs that of male–male conflicts. Further, women stalking women far outweighs that of men stalking men. When a man walks into a nightclub, he is very likely to scan the room and look at the women first; when a female walks into a nightclub, she will generally look at other women first too. In other words, women may regard other women as potential competition. One explanation for the level of female–female stalking may be that although women are slowly being given better work opportunities, a fewer proportion of them gain senior positions than men and this may create more situations of conflict, threat and tension between women in the workplace. Onlookers may perceive this conflict as just a common spat between two women who are equally participating, but it can often be a bullying situation. This can then lead to further distress for the victim because the bullying behaviour is not taken seriously and the target does not receive the support they need.'

There is no evidence about whether the stalker has a conscience, says Troy McEwan. 'A more psychological question is whether stalkers have issues with empathy. Again, there has been little research done on this but, based on my experience and on research with other offender groups (such as sexual or violent offenders), I think that people who stalk probably would not have broad empathy deficits. Rather, I think it is much more about getting so caught up in their own wants, needs and desires, and the very strong emotions that go with these things, that they stop thinking about the impact on the other person. Of course, there are also cases in which the purpose of the stalking is very clearly to cause harm, but even in these cases, it is unlikely that the stalker has a general empathy deficit. Usually it is much more specific than that – they specifically might not be empathising with the victim because, in their head, they believe that the harm they are causing is justified by the perceived harm the victim has caused them. That of course doesn't excuse or justify their behaviour at all, but it goes some way towards explaining it.'

Stalking strangers

The stalking of celebrities and public figures does differ in some ways from stalking of people who are directly known to the perpetrator, but it is a matter of degree rather than being a completely different phenomenon. Certainly, those who stalk celebrities are in many ways similar to people who stalk strangers who are not celebrities. Stranger stalkers generally experience much higher rates of severe mental illness than other stalkers, and the symptoms often directly contribute to the stalking. This is particularly true of those who target public figures. Most of what we know about stalking of celebrities comes from studies of people who stalk and harass royalty or politicians; this work has shown that as many as four out of five people who target members of the British royal family seem to suffer from severe forms of mental illness. Similarly, in Troy McEwan's experience of working with stalkers who have targeted public figures, such as newsreaders, politicians and sportspeople, she has found their behaviour has usually been driven by either delusional beliefs about the target (for example, that they are related to them or have a relationship with them), or a severe personality disorder that leads the stalker to misinterpret their relationship with the public figure. This means that in these cases a central aspect of stopping the stalking behaviour is helping the stalker to access appropriate psychiatric and psychological treatment so that the mental disorder that is contributing to their behaviour can hopefully be resolved.

Why do people stalk others?

Stalking can arise from a multitude of situations and can be perpetrated by all sorts of people.

The most common kinds of situations that contribute to stalking are those that cause very strong negative emotions – usually associated with a sense of mistreatment and betrayal. This might be associated with an ex-partner, but equally could involve a service provider, a neighbour or even a stranger. Ex-partner stalking can also be motivated by strong feelings of anxiety and sadness at the end of the relationship, with the stalking being a desperate attempt to resume the relationship rather than have to face its loss. The other, less common, kind of situation is one in which the stalker perceives the victim in a very positive way and the stalking – at least initially – is motivated by positive feelings, such as hope that a relationship might start, happiness at having found someone, and so on.

Most people who stalk seem to do it only once in their life. Research shows that around one-third of stalkers reoffend with further stalking, about half targeting a new victim and half the same victim as they have before. Although this is concerning, it does mean that about two-thirds do not go on to do it again. It really is something about the situation in which the stalking started and continued that contributes to the behaviour, and changing that situation can stop them from stalking again.

> Dr Rachel MacKenzie is an internationally recognised expert in the field of stalking, having conducted research in the area, being widely published and working with both victims and perpetrators of stalking for many years. When assessing a stalker, one of the questions she asks is 'What did you hope to achieve?' Rachel says that when assessing the stalker in a forensic setting, it is rare that they have achieved the goal that first underpinned the harassment.

Stalking by proxy

Some stalkers, particularly those with resentful motives, will start campaigns that draw in others who become involved in harassing the victim. These stalking-by-proxy actions can vary from things like petitions and complaints to much more personal and terrifying strategies. 'One particular strategy that I am familiar with,' says Troy McEwan, 'both from cases I have worked with and cases that have been written about in the media, is posting information about the victim's whereabouts on online chat forums and encouraging others to make contact with them. I know of a few cases in which the stalker has put the victim's home address on sites for those with unusual sexual interests, with messages such as "Come on over to my house". People from the site will then unwittingly appear at the target's house, causing, at the very least, considerable embarrassment to the victim and, at the worst, outright fear of sexual assault. In one case, the stalker was targeting a professional whom she believed had done a poor job for her. She found a website for people with similar complaints about others and posted the victim's work address, suggesting that those on the website might help her in her harassment.'

These kinds of campaigns can be particularly damaging for professionals. Often they will be accompanied by complaints to registration boards or other agencies to whom the professional is beholden. Such agencies are obliged to investigate any complaints, meaning that the victim is then required to answer endless complaints, sometimes from different bodies and sometimes over years, with real consequences for their career. In one case Troy McEwan cites, a series of complaints was made about the victim over the course of two years, by which point the victim had responded to complaints made to four different bodies, both internal to her employer and to external review agencies, including a state-based complaints body. Each complaint had been found to be groundless, yet every subsequent body was still obliged to investigate. This kind of vexatious complaining is absolutely a tool of resentful stalkers and is sometimes poorly understood by the agencies reviewing the complaints, thus exacerbating the effects on the victims.

Cyberstalking

With all the positives that the internet brings in connecting people and creating easy communication, if these same features are used maliciously it can cause considerable damage. Stalking has always involved attempts to damage the target's reputation – for example, in one case a stalker posted derogatory leaflets about the victim across an entire country town; in another the victim's workplace was graffitied with slanderous slogans. When these kinds of strategies are employed online, their potential to genuinely harm the victim is vastly increased, both at the time and in the future. Stalkers use the internet in various ways to damage targets' reputations. Perhaps the most common and easiest way is to publish compromising photographs of the victim – usually sexual, sometimes manipulated. This often happens via social media, sometimes through the stalker's own account, but also by infiltrating and posting them on the victim's page so they are exposed to all their friends and family. Other techniques stalkers use include emails sent around workplaces and creating websites about the target.

The damage caused to a target's reputation by cyberstalking can be long-term – years after material has been posted on the internet it can still be retrieved through searches. Search engines and social media sites are beginning to get better at blocking or closing these kinds of avenues, but they are often far too slow to respond to complaints and, meanwhile, the damage has often already been done. These kinds of acts are criminal and they should be reported to police. It is essential that victims take screenshots of the pages, as embarrassing as that can be, because the police will not be able to act without physical evidence.

Who is targeted?

There have been studies around the world looking at the prevalence of stalking victimisation, with most suggesting that somewhere around 15 per cent of people experience being stalked at some time in their lives, with rates of 17 to 30 per cent for women and 4 to 12 per cent for men. There is no evidence that stalking is increasing in frequency – although there was a definite increase in stalking recorded by police throughout the 1990s and into the early 2000s, that was probably because it had just been recognised as a crime.

Relatively little research has been conducted on age and stalking. Younger people (adolescents and young adults) do seem more likely to become targets of stalking, which may reflect their greater likelihood of becoming victims of crime. It also might be that they are exposed to more situations that can engender stalking, such as more frequent relationship seeking and dissolution. One study looked at the age of victim and stalker pairs, which showed that people tend to be stalked by those of similar age to them, although as the stalkers got older (over 60), they were equally likely to stalk same-age peers or younger acquaintances. This study also suggested that older victims were more likely to experience physical violence during the stalking episode, which goes against general findings that younger people are more physically violent as a group. There is also some evidence to suggest that a greater proportion of adolescent stalkers are female – possibly because there are fewer ex-partner stalkers in this young group.

Chapter 2

How Victims Are Affected

Stalking has devastating consequences for the victims. The behaviour is often misunderstood and the targets often don't know how to express what is happening to them. Often even their caring friends and family can be confused about what is taking place. The fear, anxiety and stress of being stalked can consume the victim's life, affecting their self-confidence, relationships and careers. It can lead to physical harm, including suicide and murder. Many victims move house; some change their phone number, their name or their occupation. Some do all of the above in the hope of escaping. Although not all stalking victims will suffer these terrible outcomes, many do, highlighting the fact that stalking needs to be dealt with as a serious behaviour and a serious offence.

Dr Lorraine Sheridan is a world-renowned forensic psychologist, who focuses on applied intervention and investigating stalking crimes. 'Think about everything you do in your life – the amount of time you invest in your studies, your home life, your relationships, going food shopping, to the football game,' she says. 'All that time, all that effort, and more, a stalker can put into targeting one person and making that person's life a misery. Only when you think about it like that will you really understand what a stalker can do.'

In 1996, when Lorraine Sheridan was an undergraduate student, England and Wales were about to outlaw stalking and she thought that it would be an interesting topic for a final-year project. She went on to complete a PhD and write a book on stalking and she continues to undertake research into the subject.

She was also interested in the psychological aspects of stalking because she knew someone who was being targeted. 'I began by looking at what stalking actually is because it is really hard to define. In fact, there is no precise legal definition of stalking. However, if the behaviour that constitutes stalking were clearly defined the perpetrators would do something else to get around the law. They can be very ingenious. Another complication is that stalking is chronic rather than acute – in other words, on average it lasts six to eight months, whereas most interpersonal crimes, like rape, muggings and burglary, are one-off events. The longest stalking case I've worked on lasted 43 years, and then the stalker went on to target the original victim's daughter.'

As well as research, Lorraine Sheridan has worked with British and Australian police as an offender profiler. 'Many of the cases recorded by police as an index crime – murder, rape and attempted murder – are in fact stalking because of the accumulation of events leading up to the crime and even occurring afterwards. But stalking is difficult to recognise.' Lorraine Sheridan has worked with the police on how to recognise stalking, developing a checklist that helps them ask the right questions, collect the right evidence and identify which cases may be most likely to lead to violence or culminate in murder.

The stereotypical stalker is the dark shadowy weirdo, socially isolated, hanging around alleyways. They can be that but, as Lorraine Sheridan points out, they can also be well-adjusted, handsome, wealthy people, respected members of society such as doctors or lawyers, and they can be male or female. One defining characteristic is that, along with people who commit fraud, stalkers are more likely to be of higher socioeconomic status than most criminals. There is no compelling reason why they stalk – it seems to be just because they can.

Research results

The impact of stalking on victims' lives has been the subject of a lot of research studies. One of the first was done in the 1990s by Michele Pathé, collecting information from stalking victims she was treating. In this group, 39 per cent moved house as a result of the stalking, 53 per cent changed or ceased their employment, and all but six people out of 100 made significant changes to their social and work lives. In the same study, the participants reported that they suffered marked psychological impacts from the stalking, with high levels of anxiety reported by four out of five respondents, and nightmares, depressed mood, appetite disturbance and intrusive memories by many. One quarter reported that they had thought about suicide as a direct result of being stalked. In all the years that have passed since this study, a wide range of other research has been done around the world finding consistent results.

Lorraine Sheridan conducted a major study of 2000 stalking targets, who completed a wide-ranging 50-page questionnaire. The people who are targeted are usually stable, safe and intelligent, but the results showed how deeply stalking affected their lives. The social, physical and emotional effects have been well documented, but the true extent of these effects may not be known. The most shocking finding was that 45 per cent of respondents reported having considered suicide. This does not take into account the number of people who had been the target of stalkers and had been driven to kill themselves.

The research also highlighted that an average of 43 people are drawn into each stalking case. It is not just the person being targeted who are adversely affected, but their children, parents, friends, neighbours and work colleagues may be directly impacted by the stalking. This is one of the most confronting effects of stalking, Lorraine Sheridan says.

'And the people around you, your friends, your colleagues, do not understand what is happening. The common belief is that it's just someone interested in you and all you need to do is tell them to go away. In psychology we call that the "just-world hypothesis", which is the assumption that the world is fair and nothing bad will happen to you. If it does, then this must be the consequence of you acting badly. So, for example, if you had a relationship with the stalker, people will believe that you must have done something to the stalker and you are "getting what you deserve" and, in some way, the moral balance is being restored.' The police or help services commonly tell victims: 'Do not respond to the stalker under any circumstances'. But what if the stalker is threatening your children, what if the stalker tells lies about you to make you lose your job? What if the stalker is phoning you 60 times a day – and if you answer on the 61st phone call, you are responding. Then of course the victim will be told, 'You shouldn't have responded'. But it is human nature to react and try to stop the stalking.

Finding fault with the victim means that people can blame the victim and thus maintain their belief in a just and fair world.

It is not that the victims do not blame themselves. Although, as is the stereotype, four out of five targets are women, a significant number of men are victims of stalking and they too 'are ashamed and emasculated by the stalking'. Lorraine Sheridan recalled a man who 'had been a boss in the paratroopers, had led night raids, worked in the really scary parts of Iraq, held people while they died and picked up bits of his comrades blown all over the road. The woman who stalked him weighed 50 kilograms and absolutely ruined his confidence. He had never been so terrified and he couldn't report it. He was too frightened.'

The extraordinarily high financial costs of being stalked are also often ignored. Targets have to deal with vandalism, security measures, legal and healthcare expenses directly related to the stalking, and they sometimes lose their jobs and their livelihoods. There are some who have lost millions because they were stalked.

Long-term stalking

The psychopathic stalker who will hunt somebody and make targeting them their whole life, is very unusual. Lorraine Sheridan describes a case of a man stalking another man, both students at university. The target was well-adjusted and successful. The perpetrator, who was an odd, socially isolated individual, harassed the other student, displaying jealousy and hatred for no apparent reason. He spread a lot of lies about him, including that he was a paedophile, and even attempting to get him thrown out of the university. On graduation day the stalker said to the target, 'I know you well, golden boy. You will make a success of your life but I will come back and ruin it. You'll see me in 20 years.' Twenty years to the day, the target watched a man walk down his driveway. It was the stalker. He introduced himself and said, 'I didn't get caught last time and I'm not going to get caught again. I have plans for you and I'm just going to take my time.' But the law and the times had changed. The target went to the police and the stalker was convicted of the criminal offence of credible threat. He is still being watched for possible stalking.

This is one case Lorraine Sheridan says she thinks about in the middle of the night. 'This one bothers me. I hope I don't hear anything more about it.' This is an example of the kind of stalker – 'and thankfully there are very few of them' – who will stop at nothing. They don't care about anything else and are happy to die in their cause, as if they were suicide bombers. They are so good at 'playing the victim', at convincing others they have been wronged, that even in jail they will get prison officers and the most hardened criminals on their side. In such circumstances, Lorraine Sheridan says. 'You can identify the risk but if they have not actually committed a crime, there is not a lot you can do.' You can't arrest someone for something they might be going to do.

Chapter 3

Targeting the Young

'When I was a young girl I would escape into what I felt was a safe place, the garden. It was a little garden but there were trees, and I would find a place in the vegetable patch and lie there. Maybe it was just nature that gave me that beautiful feeling, or a smell. I naturally felt at one and the energy was the complete opposite of the energy inside our house. After an incident when my mother targeted and bullied me, just ten minutes in this quiet natural space would rejuvenate me. Sometimes I would follow ants around on the path wondering where they were going. This ignited my curiosity. When I was alone in the garden, I did not feel the isolation and non-inclusion, which was echoingly lonely for a little child.'

Valerie was relentlessly bullied by her mother all through her childhood. In the 1950s when Valerie was a child, such behaviour was swept under the carpet, but today, in a number of jurisdictions, repeated acts of bullying are classified under the criminal offence of stalking. The terms 'bullying' and 'stalking' are often interchanged, particularly when referring to behaviours involving cyberspace, and we tend to call unwanted and unwelcome behaviour bullying when it involves children, but stalking when adults are the targets. There are differences, many of them involving the motivation, persistence and personality of the perpetrator, but bullying and stalking share many common elements, including: invading someone's personal space; intimidation and control; direct, intense and overtly threatening behaviour, and disruptive – and sometimes violent – forms of pursuit. A 2009 study published in the *British Journal of Psychiatry* concluded that the link between bullying and stalking is often ignored.

'I had a brother who was four years younger and during all this time it was my job to look after him – it did not matter how badly she abused me, I still had to look after my brother,' Valerie says. 'I don't know how I got through it. I was a quiet child and feared judgement because I was accused of so many things that I did not do but was punished for anyway.' From a very young age, she taught herself how to endure her mother's relentless targeting. 'My family was not religious, but I had this spiritual part of my being. I even remember pre-verbally calling out to God, *Help*, in a terrified voice that echoed through me. I always felt an energetic presence and it is still with me. It is a graceful, calming energy.'

Valerie's father was also traumatised by her mother – 'I learned later that a psychiatrist had told him: "Your wife is capable of either killing you or your daughter." When I was 11, I remember asking him, "Dad, why don't you leave?" He replied: "I can't leave because you three children are my responsibility." I cannot begin to explain the relief I felt at that moment.

'Dad was a very funny man, a lovely person. He definitely

feared for my welfare. My mother was beating me constantly and Dad was working shift work and was worried about my physical and emotional survival. "Please keep trying to look at the funny side," he would say. I kept thinking that I couldn't see the funny side of having the shit being beaten out of me, but I would go somewhere in my head and try and find somewhere lighter to be. That taught me about optimism – even though it sounded really stupid at the time, Dad was trying to help me survive.'

When Valerie was 17, her mother died. 'I had a lot of healing to do and I did that through developing my curiosity and conquering my fears.' As a teenager, her mother had prevented Valerie from continuing her education. But now she went to university and during this time met her future husband. When he asked her to marry him, 'I said to be careful because "My mother could be lying dormant in me." He fell on the couch laughing, holding his stomach, saying I must be joking. He gave me the courage to face my greatest fear – which was to become a mother. When I saw my baby for the first time, I knew I was not like my mother. I knew my daughter was the most precious being.'

Bullying can cause severe psychological distress. Valerie describes her mother's unpleasant and often violent targeting as 'damaging to the soul'. She spent years recovering. 'One of the things that more than anything helped me stop the racket in my head was meditation. It was something I have found extremely positive and I found that it promotes optimism as well.'

An unequal balance of power is common to all types of bullying and stalking – in Valerie's case an adult pursuing a child, but among children often an outsider, someone who is different, is targeted by their more conformist peers.

Aunty Joy Murphy, now in her senior years, is a proud senior Aboriginal elder of the Wurundjeri people. 'I loved going to primary school. We lived in a family home just two hills from school. My beautiful Prince, a grey whippet, would walk with me to school and then be waiting for me at the gate at the end of the day. The first hill prepared you for the second big hill. Most of the kids were great but every now and then there would be someone who was just simply nasty and called us "blackie" and "dirty". The teacher knew but never took any action. The headmaster also did nothing. When my sister and I were upset and said we were not going back to school, our mum would put the two younger brothers in the heavy pram and we would have to help her push the pram up the hills. Our mother was so strong in many ways.

'One day, my Prince was not at the gate. I ran home crying. Prince was gone. Soon after that, someone called me "dirty blackie". I ran out of the classroom and back home. Our front door was on the footpath. When you opened the door, all you could see was a shining floor that you could eat your food on. I ran straight through the house to outside where the washing was done. I grabbed the pumice stone and scraped both my elbows until they bled – funnily, they are still the blackest skin of my body. I ran past Mum, blood dripping on her clean floor, back to the school straight into the headmaster's office. He was dumbfounded and I made sure my blood dripped all over his desk.

'That day changed my life. My blood is not a different colour and is as good as anyone's. When my father was dying,

I asked him to leave me something. He said, "You are who you are, be proud of who you are but you are no better than anyone else." And we are as good as anyone.'

Being different was also the catalyst for bullying experienced by public servant Antoinette Khalil, who immigrated to Australia with her family from Egypt when she was six years old. 'I had the privilege and good fortune to grow up in a loving and caring family with parents who were totally dedicated to providing a happy and safe family home environment for my sister and me,' she says. 'The word bullying was not a word that I was familiar with as a child. It is not a word that even when translated in my own mother tongue, Egyptian, makes any sense to me. Maybe it is because it was not something that I did so I did not give much consideration to as a child. I do have olive skin and curly dark hair, which was not so trendy in primary school or high school. I was called "Gollywog", my Greek, Macedonian and Italian friends were called "wogs" and "dagos". We didn't know then that racist names or having the boys make fun of me by doing what they thought was an Egyptian dance was bullying. No one gave this type of behaviour a name. No one addressed it.

'I consider myself fortunate not to have been psychologically or emotionally impaired by this and to have grown up to have a rewarding and fulfilling life,' she says. 'Bullying can leave a young child or adult scared and damaged potentially for life. We know only too well the tragedies that have occurred in the lives of many, young and old alike, who have been subjected to bullying – an act that has eaten away at the very depth of their heart, soul and spirit, leaving only a shell. Without bullies what a safer world it would be.'

Antoinette Khalil was fortunate to overcome the bullying behaviour she experienced. But often, as lawyer Tony Carbone says, 'people who have been bullied just bottle up their feelings and suffer in silence'. The actor Tony Bonner believes that 'what we witnessed, what we felt, during our childhood unfortunately seeped into the essence of self. Then we have spent our adult life attempting to repair that period. We had to come to an understanding that "it wasn't our fault".'

Norman Schueler, deputy chairman of the South Australian Multicultural and Ethnic Affairs Commission, believes that, 'Bullying behaviour which can be violent, aggressive, verbal, emotional and coercive has a crushing impact on the victim. The isolation, despair and distress of a bullying relationship cause pain and scars. One university student, who was being bullied and didn't have anyone to talk to about it, described the experience as thinking that there was no end in sight, that it would never cease. It felt like a car that had been in a traffic accident, she said, and despite all the garage and repair work to the body and engine, it still didn't drive the same as it did beforehand.'

Psychologist Gary Rubin explains that, like all other behaviours, bullying can be learned and can continue indefinitely. It may be either witnessed or experienced at home or be a projection of repressed emotions. Children who bully have often experienced some form of trauma or difficulty themselves – they may witness or experience bullying at home or their behaviour is a projection of repressed emotions. And 'the behaviour that starts in childhood can turn into something more disturbing', Gary Rubin says.

Former MP Leonie Hemingway says that, 'Bullying has

always seemed to me like an assault of irony. Emotionally, the bully is always the smaller person, masking their own hidden weaknesses by exploiting those more obvious in the victim. But, given time, the tables turn, and the bully must look inwards to confront the emotions that enrage them. And with support, the bullied can live to find their own strength, the kind they never knew was inside them all along.'

'Bullying has an extremely adverse effect on society, and can have long-term consequences on a person's wellbeing. It's important that children, in particular, feel safe and respected at school and that schools have the resources to help the children who need it most,' says MP Michael Sukkar.

Many children are scared to go to school for fear of being bullied. Twelve-year-old Leigh says he has seen a lot of bullying at school: 'There are kids who push other kids around, not speaking very nicely and calling them terrible names. It makes the kids very upset and feeling as if they don't belong and like they want to hide in a corner. I think the schools should be helping the kids, punishing the kids who bully. They should teach us about bullying – how to cope with it, so you know what to do and what not to do – and help those who are bullied. Being isolated and bullied can lead to kids killing themselves, which is tragic.'

Leigh's ten-year-old sister Tilley experienced bullying at school. 'This girl was being mean to me and she had a group of three or four girls who, I guess, were her helpers and were doing it to make them feel more popular. They are the prettiest, the coolest girls in our grade. They would always be nice to me to my face and then they would belittle me behind my back. It made me feel sad. I just didn't want to be at the school.

Sometimes I would come home crying because it was so bad. I tried to handle it but the words and what they had done to me made me feel so upset. Sometimes when I walked past them they would shoulder-bump me – sometimes it would hurt and sometimes it wouldn't – and if I fell over they would laugh and that made me feel uncomfortable.

'I shouldn't have been put in that position. I should have felt happy, not sad. This kept on going and I told the teacher. But the mean girls didn't stop. I told myself, they're doing that to make me feel uncomfortable. So I avoided them.'

A school counsellor has helped Tilley deal with the bullying. 'He has given me a lot of advice – like, "The bullies are trying to make you feel uncomfortable but what they say is not true." So I have always had that in my head when they say something that makes me feel uncomfortable. If I am able to walk past those girls and be like, "Hi", then that will make them feel that what they are doing is just not working. Now that I have been seeing the counsellor I feel more confident to deal with all of that. I have learned that they can think what they want to, but I am going to go on with my life and not care about what they are doing.'

Tilley had the support of her family, friends and school. But others are not so fortunate, particularly if they have been subjected to cyberbullying.

For today's young person, there is an alternate reality, a virtual world created by the internet. 'We are aware of the ever-growing presence of cyberbullying that people of all ages, and in particular children, face today,' Gary Rubin says. 'The intensity of public and social scrutiny and humiliation has led to concerning increases in the rates of suicide and self-harm in adolescents.' Cyberbullying can strip the victim of self-esteem, confidence, destroy their reputation and, chillingly, in some instances even tell them that they don't deserve to live.

The tragic story of 13-year-old Libby Bell is well known in Australia. Libby was a champion junior lifesaver who appeared to be happy and confident. But in fact she was struggling to cope with years of physical abuse and cyberbullying, which took the form of regular slurs and nasty messages over Facebook, Instagram and Snapchat. Eventually the constant taunting and mocking became too much and Libby killed herself.

It has been estimated that one in five young people are targets of cyberbullies – which means that a vast number of their peers are engaging in this type of behaviour. Many children – and adults – would never be involved in 'real-life' bullying, yet they unthinkingly take part in cyberbullying, not recognising that their actions can have very real and devastating consequences for their targets.

Like many young bullying victims, Libby suffered in silence, keeping the torment she was experiencing to herself. There are a number of useful websites that describe techniques parents can use to get their children to share their feelings and describe what they are experiencing; see pages 143-158.

Prevention programs in schools are invaluable in teaching children how to recognise bullying and how to respond to it. 'Putting programs in place in schools so children learn when they are young that bullying is not okay at any level, including intimidation via the keyboard,' is really important, says politician Adrian Pederick. Such programs can also enlighten the perpetrators. As MP Kim Wells says, 'Some people don't even realise that they are committing an abuse and that's why it's crucial for young boys and girls to be taught, primarily at home but also in schools, that any form of abuse must never be tolerated.'

Learning about safety in cyberspace must be part of such programs. Communications expert Jane Speechley says she is 'alarmed to see this most cruel and insidious aspect of human behaviour proliferate, especially through social media and digital communication. Learning of the experiences of those whose stories are told in this book – and others whose stories have not yet been shared – is heartbreaking. More of us need to recognise bullying when it happens and to find the courage to speak up. Bullying thrives in the darkness. Secrecy, embarrassment and self-doubt are its oxygen. If we all turn on the lights, and call bullying by its name when we see it taking place, that alone can be enough to stop a bully in their tracks. More importantly, it helps let the target know what they're experiencing is real, it's part of a wider phenomenon, and it's a behavioural problem of the bully – not them.'

As Adam Centorrino, CEO and board member of Bully Zero Australia Foundation, says, 'Bullying touches the lives of so many in our society yet it's only recently that it has been recognised by law as a form of abuse. We must work as a community to stamp out all forms of bullying, especially given that, through the advent of technology, it no longer stops when our children leave the school yard or workplace.'

Peter Mayall, principal of accountancy firm Crowe Horwath, agrees and emphasises that everyone needs 'to stand up and not remain silent, but to say "No" to bullying behaviour and support the thousands of victims who have been subjected to this cruel abuse. In schools, workplaces, across the internet or in domestic situations bullying can no longer be tolerated, so we need to unite together to eradicate this disturbing behaviour.'

Part II

Chapter 4

Lies and Accusations

Talking to Meg, you can sense that her vulnerability and trustfulness made her the perfect target for the predator who pursued her. Even now, as she continues to build a new life in a new city, she is almost apologetic, trying to accept some of the guilt and blame for the stalking. At the same time, it is obvious she believes she is lucky – many women in situations similar to hers have not escaped with their lives.

Meg was in her early 30s when she met Paul at a New Year's Eve party. 'My friends knew him and I thought he seemed nice,' she says. 'He talked about angels, and I believe in angels, so we hit it off. The next day he called and we arranged to meet. I took a girlfriend along and the three of us had a fun night out on the town. But my intuition was telling me that something wasn't quite right about him. He seemed moody but, at least at the beginning, he said all the right things. And because he knew my other friends, I gave him a little bit more credence. So I decided he was okay.'

A few days later, Paul called Meg and they went out for drinks. 'Even though I was blown away by the excitement of a possible relationship, I remember him talking about sex, what he liked to do in bed. I am not a prude but part of me was thinking, *Wow, hang on, you've only just met me.* I kept thinking, *Hey, this isn't right.* But there was also part of me saying, *I want to be loved, I want to be in a relationship.*'

They arranged to meet again. Just before the appointed time she caught up with a male friend. This made Paul very angry with Meg and he stormed off, leaving her in the pub on her own. 'I look back now and I think that was the warning sign,' Meg says. 'But, of course, the next day when he called and said, "I'm so sorry. I did it because I'm developing feelings for you and I really like you", that was what I really wanted to hear. At the time it was exciting. I'd been bored and I guess I saw him as a project.'

The relationship was very intense, very passionate, and the sex was good. 'But one minute everything would be great and the next thing I was in trouble – it could be for anything – and he would storm off and leave me. The message was clear – either you do what I want you to do or you won't see me – and I wanted to see him so much. I think I got very needy.' Whenever they met, Meg would behave very cautiously. 'I started to notice that I was walking on egg shells. I knew if I behaved well and was a "nice girl", he would show me some attention and love, which is what I really wanted. I would be grateful if he spent a few nights a week with me – even if he was awful to me on Sunday, Monday, Tuesday, I would be so excited that I got to see him on a Wednesday. I remember the number of times he let me down at the last minute and I would be heartbroken. I wasn't very resilient then and took it personally, thinking, *It's me. I must be doing something wrong.* I spent so much time trying to change the way I was around him, instead of recognising that his behaviour was not acceptable. And all his friends said he was a great guy, a fabulous guy, so the relationship just continued.'

The stalking began in earnest the first time Meg tried to leave Paul. She had heard someone talking about unhealthy relationships and what an abusive relationship was and 'I thought to myself, *Oh my god, that is me, that is absolutely me.*' Meg sat down and said to Paul, 'This isn't working for me.' He cried and begged her to change her mind. She refused.

'The first couple of days were okay, but then I switched on my mobile phone and there were 50 text messages. And I had over 60 emails from him. Although I knew what he was doing was wrong, there was still a huge part of me that wanted to be loved. People like Paul have a knack of knowing your hot spots and what to say to get you down – "You are my only love", "I love you so much – that's why I am doing this", "I'm so sorry, it won't happen again". He would change and things were going to be different, he'd say. I wanted to believe him, so of course I fell for it and went back.'

Meg got into a cycle of trying to leave. 'I tried seven times and every time he inundated me with phone calls, text messages, emails. He would arrive at my place at three in the morning, banging on the door. Or he would turn up outside my work crying his eyes out. Of course I didn't want to see him upset, so I would agree to try again.' Or he would turn up with a big bouquet of flowers, catching her at a low point, and say, 'I'm so sorry. I have spent the last six months healing myself and trying to get better.' He was seeing a counsellor and would adopt the language he had learned there: 'I know that

I'm acting this way because I am adopted.' 'I know that it's because I love you so much.' Again, Paul was appealing to the part of Meg that really wanted the relationship to work. She would try it one more time. 'It would be great for two weeks but then go downhill.'

Meg came to dread splitting up with Paul because it involved going through this dark process. 'I really didn't like myself very much and I also didn't like the fact that I couldn't seem to break away from him,' she says. 'It was almost easier to stay than it was to get away. The getting away was such hard work. Every day I would get irrational messages from him – "You left because you're pregnant", "You left because you're having an affair with somebody else". The natural thing is to defend yourself, to say this is ridiculous, but you can't because it's like he's talking at cross purposes.' And Paul was exhibiting all the signs of the rejected stalker type, telling his friends a completely different story. 'They thought I was the nutter. That hurt, it really did hurt. I remember walking down the street one day and thinking, *I can't get away from this person and I want to. I need to but I can't. He will not let me get away. What am I going to do?* I went to see my doctor and said, "Please help me do whatever it is I need to do to keep away from this person".

'By this time I had learned not to respond. I even changed my phone number, but he would always find another way to contact me. Turning up at work, calling me at work. The text messages did my head in more than anything. I would try to ignore them, but I'd switch off my phone at night and in the morning there would be all these dinging alerts of messages coming through – 50 to 100 messages a day. I'd wake up thinking, *Oh god, what is going to happen today?* I would have to deal with his physical presence too. One of my friends worked on the ferry service and he would tip me off if Paul was waiting for me to go through the ticket barrier. I had no way to escape – it was the only way through. Another friend would meet me on the ferry every day but Paul would still follow me. If I was in a restaurant, he would sit in the restaurant the whole time.'

As Meg says, 'It's the constant emotional battering that wears you down. It's difficult when someone is harassing you and he is sitting across from you crying his eyes out, saying he loves you. Or I would get a phone call saying, "I'm going to kill myself".'

Once, when they were apart, Meg got sick. 'This part of my life was horrific,' she says. 'I ended up in hospital for an operation. I came around from the anaesthetic at 2pm in the afternoon, so none of my friends was there. But he was. Somehow he'd found out where I was. Part of me was glad that someone was there. The other part was looking for the nearest scalpel.

'I was at my most vulnerable. He knew exactly how to play me,' Meg says. Paul invited her to recuperate at his house, promising to look after her. When they got there, 'he refused to let me in his living room. He threw me into the bedroom and told me I needed to stay in there. I asked for a glass of water and he threw it at me. I was feeling lower and lower, but I also had this fear about what would happen if I tried to leave. I was numb. I couldn't feel anything anymore. I didn't know who I was. I was just being what he wanted me to be. I wanted to leave but I didn't know how to do it.

'I was getting sicker and sicker and was taking time off work. My friends had good intentions, but they said, "Why don't you just leave?" As if I hadn't tried.'

Meg had never taken drugs until she met Paul, but she began taking ecstasy so she could block out the bad experiences and reduce the panic she was experiencing. She submerged her own personality in order to keep him happy and to keep the peace. This leaving-and-making-up pattern went on for about five years. 'I used to dream of leaving him,' she says. 'I remember towards the end he was walking up the stairs behind me and I was thinking how much I really hated him. But I was too scared to actually make the break.'

A friend, who loathed Paul, sat Meg down one day and said, 'What's going on? Can I help you?' She understood his nature and was supportive, intercepting his phone calls. But even that didn't stop the messages or emails. 'The emails were unbelievable,' Meg says. 'I kept them for a while in case there was any sort of trouble. I did think about going to the police, but I didn't want to, particularly since he had a child who I didn't want to suffer in any way.'

Finally, a friend who had also been in a toxic relationship said, 'Get out of it. Come and live with me.' Something snapped that day, Meg says. 'I thought, *Yes*. I didn't tell him but I packed up all my stuff and went to live with her, which was a safe space. I think that was when he knew I was really serious.'

At this point the stalking really escalated. 'The text messages continued and he would call me at my office. "I'm outside your work," he'd say. "You need to come and see me, I'm really upset. If you don't come out, I'm going to take my own life." I tried taking different routes to work but he would be there, standing outside my office. As soon as I got into work, the messages would start: "What are you doing?" "Who have you been out with?" "Why didn't you answer my calls last night?" "Why didn't you do this – you must be up to something." "I know what you're doing and what you're up to." "You're pregnant." "How could you do this to me?" The phone would ring, then it would go dead. There were blocked messages, calls from other people's phones. It was exhausting.'

Despite the constant harassment, Meg was feeling a little stronger. She was still living with her friend and an old male friend from her home town came and stayed with them for a while. He was good company and Meg enjoyed having him around. She kept away from Paul, switching off her phone and deleting messages as soon as they came in – which caused him to panic and consequently she would be deluged with more and more text messages and emails.

Paul got his friends involved. They were ringing Meg, saying how sad he was and that he wanted to see her: 'He said you left and he is devastated.' At the same time, Paul was badgering Meg, saying if she didn't want him, then he would go off with someone else. When he put his profile up on a dating website, he included the comment, 'I wouldn't have to be on here if it wasn't for you and you know who you are', and sent Meg the link. One time, he turned up to a club when Meg was there and told everyone that he loved her. He gave her clothes and presents. 'Then he sent me some tickets for a Neale Donald Walsch event with a letter saying, "I don't mind if you take someone else", so I did. I took a friend, he was just a friend. The next day I got a message from Paul saying, "You went with X – how could you do this to me?" '

This bullying continued for three or four months and, says Meg, was 'the worst it had ever been. I couldn't go anywhere. I was on tenterhooks all the time. Friends walked me out of the building each night, friends met me on the way to work. I had to learn not to take him on. His and my realities were completely different – it was like talking in a different language. You expect people to be reasonable, to listen and understand what you have to say, but when they don't, it really confuses you. It is better to not try to make them understand.'

Meg wasn't afraid of Paul hurting her physically but she was worn down by the relentless emotional and verbal abuse. His wild accusations weighed particularly heavily on her and she describes the guilt she felt when Paul accused her of ruining his life as 'dreadful'. He would say to her, 'Look at the state of me. I love you so much – how can you do this to me? Everybody leaves me – you told me you wouldn't leave me. I am nothing now, I've lost my job. I've done nothing. If you come back everything will be okay.' As Meg says, you can only take so much of 'I'm a mess and it's your fault', 'My family is worried about me and it's your fault', 'I haven't spent time with my son and it's your fault', 'I'll take my life because you're not in it and it's your fault.' She says she 'spent so long teetering around, scared about going out, not wanting to go out because he might turn up at the house or be watching me.'

Paul continued to stalk Meg with text messages. 'You think you are all right for a week,' Meg says, 'and then they would start again. It was horrible. I felt like I couldn't get away. Some days I was strong and other days I was really down. I'd think to myself, *What can I do? I can't get away, I'll never get away from this person.* I was in a daze, not sleeping, dreading what was going to happen, when or where he was going to turn up.'

Then someone said to her, 'You don't have the power to ruin his life.' She suddenly recognised the truth of that and slowly began to change how she thought about Paul and his behaviour. 'It was almost as if I needed to do something radical to get away from him. Otherwise I would have ended up dead because I was exhausted, sick, taking antidepressants. I'd think, *Maybe if I walk in front of this car, I will not have to deal with him any more.* It wasn't about my life, it was about getting away from him. Then, thankfully, one day I just thought the only way I can get rid of him is to leave the country.

'Within three weeks I'd bought tickets to visit my family. I booked a trip to Africa and then one to India because I thought he can't get me there. I blocked him on all my social media sites. But he found out I was going and turned up with presents. I was so terrified of him that I just went along with it for a couple of days. He actually took me to the airport, all the time pressuring me to promise I would come back. I felt that it was like getting away from a hostage situation. I would have told him anything because I had my ticket and I was off. I was getting away from him.

'I cried and cried on the plane. It wasn't like, now I've got away I feel great – it was not like that at all. I had been living on anxiety for so long I didn't know how to calm down. I treated myself to three nights in the best hotel in Bangkok as a I've-got-away-from-him reward. At the hotel I had eight treatments in three days and I don't think I felt any of them. No massage, no facial, no nothing. I had just switched off. It was as if my system had completely shut down.'

When her mother met Meg at the airport, she said, 'Oh my god, what has happened to you?' Time spent 'talking to my sister and to my friends really helped and so did going on a trip to somewhere completely different like Africa. I was getting in touch with my spiritual side. India was just amazing too. I started to think, *You know, I'm not that person who has been in that relationship any more. I'm teaching English to women with HIV and that's cool.* When I was walking around India and connecting with all the people there, suddenly little bits of Meg started to come out again. I thought, *You know you are all right.* I had lost myself for so long.

'Paul continued to text me but, with the time difference and the distance, it was much easier to just ignore him. I was busy and having fun.

'I spent seven months overseas and then had to decide what to do. I felt I was in a really good condition to come back. What was gratifying was that I met a couple of guys when I was travelling and it was so easy to see the red flags. I had learned a big lesson. I was not going there again. It made me determined to never be in that situation again. I knew I needed to learn to love myself again and to always recognise the warning signs. All that energy I had been putting into him needed to go into my own emotional well-being.'

Since she returned, Meg has not seen Paul. 'The last time I had contact with him was five years ago,' she says. 'I avoid him on social media. I see him on TV sometimes and I am tempted to look but, no, I'm not going there either. And I never ask about him. I don't want to know.' Several years ago, one of Meg's friends told Paul where she was. 'I haven't spoken to her since,' Meg says. 'This is about me now. It takes a long time to feel safe again. If I saw him in the street I would walk straight past. I feel sorry for anyone he meets because I actually think he has done this to other people before – because it is all about him, being abandoned, being left.'

Five years after their last contact, Meg feels totally disassociated from it all. 'But leaving an abusive partner, a stalker, is one of the most difficult things I have ever done. It is definitely harder than going through a divorce or moving overseas.'

As Meg says, stalkers do not respect your boundaries. 'It was like somebody ripped out my heart and trod all over it and gave it back,' she says. 'Don't tolerate stalking because it will eat away at your self-esteem and will leave you a shell. The best thing you can do for yourself is to get the hell out of there, get some help and support. Love yourself enough to only accept healthy people in your life.'

Chapter 5

A Crazed Fan

Mark Wilson's devastating ordeal is well known in Australia. On two separate occasions an unknown stalker set fire to his dance studios, which were burned to the ground. The perpetrator has never been found, while life for Mark and his family will never be the same. 'Whoever it was tried to destroy our lives, and I felt helpless about being able to protect my family. For us, dancing has never been a job, it's a way of life.'

When you work for a company, you are creating income for someone else and you get rewarded for that. It is different when you create something from nothing, something that gives you a real sense of fulfilment. That is what Mark and his wife Annemarie did when they began their dancing business with his brother and sister-in-law, holding dance nights attended by more than 100 children and couples.

'With dancing there are so many things that ticked boxes,' Mark says. 'There's a fitness perspective and an artistic perspective. It's a very wholesome and creative thing to do, particularly now that technology plays such a big part in youngsters' lives. Dancing gives them social skills and confidence.' Mark ran dance programs in schools: 'When the kids danced, it was like witnessing an unconscious sense of release. They reacted to the music, dancing to the rhythm. When you see them do that for the first time it feels amazing. By the time they have their second class they really want to be there. They're having fun. For us that's a real buzz. It's not just dancing – it's the social skills they learn.' Some go on to study dancing seriously and become very accomplished. 'That's exciting, seeing them progressing from one level to another from the beginner stage.' Mark has taught dancers who have gone on to be national champions or have performed in television dance shows and on stage in the musical version of *Strictly Ballroom*.

From 2004 to 2013, Mark was one of the judges on the television show *Dancing with the Stars*. Prior to that he did not have a public profile. But once the show screened, he began to recognise 'the way people become attached to you or disengaged with what you say and who they perceive you to be. There is an important PR element to being on television. You are always on show and it's important how you interact with the public.' That was 'a shock', Mark says. 'I would walk down the street and people would stop and shake my hand and say, "Hi Mark, how are you?" I'd say hi back but I wasn't sure if I actually knew them. You're not your own person any more once you're on TV. You have a public profile.'

Mark describes an evening out with his family that was typical. 'I was really exhausted – we had been travelling around doing a lot of promotional work. We went to a restaurant and hadn't even ordered our meals when a group of girls came up wanting photographs. They were taking photograph after photograph and it got to the point that Annemarie and the family were struggling to have any private conversation. We just had to become accustomed to it.'

Nevertheless, Mark was enjoying being on *Dancing with the Stars* and 'our business was going well – and it should have continued to do well. I was grateful for the opportunity. It was a new exciting world and I met so many beautiful people. I was so excited to be on television with Daryl Somers, to walk up the red carpet with the lovely Jennifer Hawkins. It was like a dream. But never in my wildest dreams did I think being on the show and having a public profile would attract the kind of attention it did.'

On Friday, 13 May 2005, seven months after *Dancing with the Stars* was first aired, there was a fire at Mark's dance studio. 'When the police phoned us, Annemarie was distraught, but I said, "Don't worry, it'll just be a small fire in the kitchen or something." I knew there was a real problem when I got to the street where the studio was and the road was blocked off. I parked the car and walked down the hill towards the fire. I could see all the windows at the top of the studio were broken and smoke was pouring out. I was hoping it was going to be okay. But the studio was completely ruined.'

It was arson. 'They used petrol or kerosene and then drizzled oil under the front door so they could use it as a slow wick and light it from the outside, which gave them time to get away. Once it got to the fuel it just took off.'

The police spent hundreds of hours interviewing and investigating possible leads. 'They conducted a very thorough investigation,' Mark says. 'I was questioned for hours. I searched my brain for someone who would have hated me to the extent that they would want to ruin my business, my life. It's very confronting when you have to go through the process of measuring your friendships against a fire. It is very unfair for the victim but it affects other people around you because their relationships with you are called into question – our teachers, other studio owners, past and present students were all under scrutiny. They were looking for anyone who may have had a grudge against us.'

Mark was desperate for answers and hired a private investigator. 'I couldn't just let it go. I wanted evidence, proof, so we could take legal action. After thousands of dollars and hundreds of hours, the investigator came up with nothing. It was enormously frustrating and overwhelming, not just for me but for all the family. Hundreds of people were impacted by the loss – the social dancers who used our dance studio as their meeting place, the competitors who lost their dance clothes valued at many thousands of dollars. The day after the fire we attended a competition and many of our dancers wore street clothing and borrowed shoes. It was soul-destroying.'

As Mark points out, it is not only the financial losses caused by a fire like this but the emotional ones. 'There were lots of autographed photographs and paintings on the studio walls which had enormous sentimental value. There were perpetual trophies from the early days of the Melbourne competition scene. We lost music that has never been converted to CD or MP3. It was all gone.

'There was a lot we had to do to just keep our heads above water and try to regain some sense of normality. It was important to keep the teachers in jobs. A woman who had a small dancewear shop at the studios was also directly affected and we had to provide an opportunity for her to continue to trade. I bought new equipment straight away, because everything had been destroyed in the fire and we held our dance classes at various venues to keep the business going – sometimes we were at three different venues a week. I was moving equipment eight hours a week – that's a normal day's work for someone.

'I was haunted … and that never leaves you. There's not a week that goes by without me thinking about what happened.'

Mark opened a new dance studio at the end of 2008. 'It was very exciting. We were one of the first studios to have plasma screens. We built a stage and installed a small lighting rig with lighting and cameras for the competitors to play back their practice (sadly not activated yet at the time of the fire). We had a fabulous barista machine and installed the Australian Dance Championship floor from Melbourne Park. It was an amazing atmosphere unlike any other studio.

Twelve weeks later Mark got a phone call. The studio had been burned down – in exactly the same way.

'The fire chief on duty rang and said, "Mark, your studio has burned down." I said he must be mistaken. "Mark," he said, "you need to get down here now."

'It was like a dream. It couldn't be happening again. I couldn't think of a single person who would want to cause me so much harm. I couldn't imagine anyone who would do this. Although the police had always thought the first fire had been targeted at me personally, I'd always found it impossible to believe. But the second fire convinced me they had to be right.' The studio had been burned in exactly the same way as the first.

'I can't begin to say how devastated I was,' Mark says.

'And so were Annemarie, our children, our teachers and our students. It was the worst time of my life.

'Somehow we had to try to keep on teaching. We used my sister-in-law's studio but we only told the people who needed to know – there was this fear of it being burned down as well. The week after the fire the stalker rang my home and told Annemarie that if we set up again they were going to burn the place down. "We know where you live," they said. "Don't set up again or we will burn your house down."

'That's when you realise your life is not your own. If someone is so determined to ruin you, to crush you, and is prepared to go to those kinds of lengths to wipe you out, financially and emotionally, there is no way you can defend yourself. I was scared stiff. I was afraid this person would come to the studio or to our home and attack us. I took my children to self-defence classes with me. If the stalking took a personally violent turn, I wanted to be able to fight long enough for Annemarie and the children to get away. I'd never been frightened in my life before. It took some getting used to.

'The sense of trust, of security, has been taken away from us. The business we were building to give to our family was gone. Not only that, but the threats meant that our ability to re-start the business again was gone.

'The police were fabulous. The guy who investigated the fire said to me, "Listen, mate, you just won't find this person." He said the stalker had made the phone call from a public phone box. It was impossible to trace him. The police had suspicions, but suspicions are not enough to go on. They said that the perpetrator will only be identified if one day he's in the pub and has a few too many drinks and boasts about the fire.'

'Mark's story serves as a reminder that irrespective of your public profile and means, a stalker is more often than not one step ahead,' lawyer Vic Rajah says. It's hard to imagine what would drive someone to cause so much pain and anguish for so many people.

'When I look back,' Mark says, 'I wonder how I coped because I was the one who had to try to put the pieces back together and get our lives on track. We were all numb with the horror of what was being done to us. I knew I had to drive the family. I'd say, we can do this and move on. So we just took the equipment that was left and moved the classes somewhere else, just moved everyone on. I knew I had to. There were teachers to consider and our students. We had to get going again.'

From his experience of the first fire Mark knew what to do immediately. 'But I was never prepared for the financial impact on our family. The stalker took away our cash flow – and also my ability to create income. It got really ugly financially. If it hadn't been for the bank we would have lost our house – they cancelled all payments and didn't ask for any money for 16 weeks.'

So many people said to Mark, 'Well, weren't you insured? The insurance will cover everything.' Yes, Mark says, 'we were insured and that paid for a lot of things. But it doesn't cover the customers who don't come back – you can't insure for that. And insurance doesn't compensate for the anxiety and insecurity your family goes through.

'And it's the ongoing fear, the tentacles of fear that spread further. It's the mothers telling us that they aren't bringing their kids back to our studio because they think it is dangerous. We'd had huge kids' classes. They just fell apart.' Nevertheless,

Mark continued the dance studio, moving around to temporary locations. 'We've been in 21 venues – we would say, this week we are going to be here, then next week we are going to move over four suburbs, and so on.'

Mark and his family also had to deal with the gossip. 'These whisperings get back to you. *He must owe money. He's had an affair and the husband found out.* There was a perception of, *Well, he's just had a second fire so he must be involved with the mafia,* or *He must have done something to someone.* It's hard to stop people wondering, stop them thinking the worst. When I would hear these kinds of stories I really didn't know what I felt. I didn't feel angry. Disappointed and frustrated, certainly, but I couldn't stop the whispering. So I focused on what I needed to do. And for me it was important to get our lives back on track.'

Mark's experiences are not uncommon for people in the public eye. 'In this case,' psychologist Gary Rubin says, 'the stalker is not one who constantly harasses or makes themselves known to their victim – in fact does the opposite.' In situations like this the perpetrator, who fits the 'resentful stalker' type, 'develops an envy or hatred towards a particular person and either wants their fame to end or to actually punish them. There are obviously a range of possible reasons why the stalker has targeted this particular victim, from the target reminding them of, or representing, someone who has impacted on them in their past or is achieving goals they themselves aspire to but have not been able to achieve. The fact that Mark had two studios burned down clearly indicates that someone really did not want him to thrive and succeed.'

One result of the stalking was that Mark did not know

who could be trusted. As Gary Rubin says, 'this could be even more destabilising as the realness and the magnitude of the trauma are intensified as a result of the physical destruction and damage to his own everyday environment.'

The stalking has changed Mark's life enormously. 'We feel unsafe. When this happens you are never ever the same. You are always wondering if that person is still out there. That angers me, but what is important is that my family know there is life beyond this. The most heartbreaking time is when the kids get angry. You can't blame them – our lives have been turned upside down.

'When you are trying to put your life back together, you are like the person at the circus spinning the plates – I had so many plates to spin and I had to make sure they wouldn't fall down. There were times when I would rock up to teach and I couldn't walk into the studio and look at one more person. So I would sit there and drink six cans of scotch and coke. That was how I tried to cope. That was hard for my wife to see – she knew I was not that person.

'But eight years of fighting to try to keep the business going took its toll. In the end we had no choice. We had to close down. We were losing money and the debt was growing. We had planned our future so carefully and it was in tatters. I was 52 and I couldn't start again. The stalker had ruined us financially. I was very angry then, which is natural. But that isn't going to solve anything. The answer is not to give up and to recognise that you have to start another life, even if this means you have to move. You have to change, adapt and reinvent yourself, which is what I did. I entered the corporate world of advertising.'

Some would say that by moving on, the stalker had won. Mark doesn't see it that way. 'Life isn't fair – it's just life – and the only way for my family and for me to regain a sense of hope was to change our lives. And as a result, many, many wonderful things have happened. It has not been an easy ride but we've grown immensely as a family. And our children have flourished and that's the most important thing to us.'

Even though Mark has moved on, he still suffers the emotional scars, trauma and financial devastation that the perpetrator cunningly inflicted on him. 'You're never really the same,' he says, 'but slowly you can grow. It does take time to let go of the past and find peace. We're not there yet. But we have a new venture and it's growing and we get to share some hope.'

Sometimes staying where you are just compounds the situation. 'You can become too scared to grow as a result of the "what ifs",' Mark says. 'Well, here are some other "what ifs". What if you got help, as we did, and started to move ahead? What if you changed the status quo and saw some light ahead that gave you just enough hope to grow again? What if you shared your story with a close friend so that someone can hold your hand and let you know you're not alone? We had friends cooking for us and bringing meals around because we couldn't buy food for ourselves. It's a very humbling experience. And it's a very loving experience to know that you're not on your own.'

Chapter 6
In the Same Business

'Social media platforms have opened up a whole new playground for would-be stalkers,' says lawyer Vic Rajah. 'A key feature of social media is sharing one's profile and personal information among a wider community. Privacy controls exist but it is very difficult to take back what is disseminated on the internet. Barbara's story is a powerful reminder that stalking may occur in many different forms.'

Barbara made contact with the man who was stalking her months before they actually met. 'It wasn't a romantic connection or anything like that. I had no inclination it would become that and it never did. He had thousands of followers on Twitter and had quite a diverse career, so I believed he was someone with a lot of connections.'

Barbara was in her mid-20s and developing her career in the same field as the stalker. 'He contacted me and said he would be interested in working together or just interested in getting into a new clique. I had been constantly assessing him, going on his news feed and seeing who he was tweeting, the work he was doing. Everything seemed legitimate. He didn't seem sleazy or anything like that – his profile looked so together and so did his website, so I thought he was fine. He said he had some PR work or writing jobs coming up, which I was interested in. We eventually met in person and he brought along Eva, a woman he had also met on Twitter and was mentoring. I introduced him to some of my business contacts. So I essentially brought him into my world.

'A couple of months down the track things started to fall apart. I realised that he wasn't that professional, that he was contacting me quite often and that he was calling me when he was in distress or had had a fight with Eva, who was the same age as I was. He had no romantic connection with her, but had been her producer/manager for about six months. He was a big dreamer and kept suggesting he had all these business opportunities and we could do this or that. But that wasn't my intention.'

Barbara had introduced him and Eva to an arts company and set up a business deal between them. 'One day I received a call from Eva, who said he had been harassing her. So I was caught in the middle. She was distressed and I really didn't know how to help her. I felt really angry. Slowly, slowly, I started reviewing his online profile and talking to a few people. It made me realise he wasn't as legitimate as he first appeared.'

Barbara is aware that it's easy to create a false online persona. 'I knew he might have been a little strange,' she says, 'but I thought he was interesting and he did have a verifiable body of work.' He was also having the kinds of conversations on Twitter that made Barbara think he was legitimate. 'Witnessing people interacting with other people online, you think everybody is friendly or sane – but it can be really false.'

She gives the example of 'a guy that my group on Twitter have all been talking to. No one has ever met him, but the fact that all of us are connected to him and chat to him regularly feels like he is part of the group. But he could turn out to be a stalker or serial killer – you don't know.'

Despite their business deal, Eva didn't want any further contact with him, but he kept contacting Barbara, asking her to talk Eva around. The more Barbara thought about it and looked at his profile, the more it seemed that he had a type: an impressionable woman her age, just starting out in the creative industry – he had a long history of getting involved with young women and promising them things. 'So I wasn't the first. He was really clever and really deceptive. He was in his 40s and he said he had a lot of connections, which he didn't. I started keeping tabs on him online – who he was contacting, who he was harassing, what he was saying about me – it was actually taking all my energy. I found he'd been ostracised from a lot of different professional organisations because he had been in trouble before. Some people in my industry regarded him as a serial pest.'

At one point an incredibly distressed Eva called Barbara, who reassured her. 'Just do this thing for the arts company,' she said. 'We have more work for you too, so don't let him try and pull the rug from under you.' One night the two women, Eva and Barbara, who had become friends through the stalking experience, went to an event connected with work. 'He showed up,' Barbara says, 'and was out the front sending text messages, not only to me and Eva but to all the people I had introduced him to in this company. He was saying things like, "Don't let them in." He caused a huge scene, sending both of us text message after text message. It was horrifically embarrassing. He was also sending texts to the company's general manager and the operations manager. He had gone online and looked up all my contacts and started contacting everyone at that particular event, everyone I had been tweeting.'

He was trying to destroy Barbara's career. 'It was really scary. I phoned him when I left the event and said, "Your behaviour was appalling, you have embarrassed me, you have contacted people I have introduced you to and tried to break down those relationships. Leave me alone, just leave me alone." He said okay, okay, and backed off. So I thought that was it. I wouldn't hear from him again.'

Several days later he sent Barbara a nasty tweet 'to say that I was a mean person to come between him and Eva. Then, after a couple of weeks, I started receiving emails, not from him but from other people. He had gone through my website, my portfolio, all my contacts on social media, and emailed anyone I had ever done work for to tell them what a bad person I was. People were contacting me saying, "What is going on? I got this strange email. What is happening?" What he had done was send a crazy, rambling email – from a man most had never met – saying that I'm a bad person. I felt really angry with myself because I had let this person have access to my life and my contacts and into my career.'

The powerful thing about stalking is that no matter how ridiculous or malevolent or crazy the stalker sounds, the victim always ends up having to defend themselves. 'You get to put on the crazy hat for a moment and it's painful,' Barbara says. She had worked hard to get work from one leading company. 'It was something I really wanted to do. I was there for two days before they got the email. As crazy as a stalker is, you always lose your dignity when you are trying to defend yourself. People feel they deserve answers. You can't just say, I'm not going to speak about it. You have to defend yourself. Otherwise you look guilty. But whatever you say, it feels inadequate. I know I am a competent and creative person, but the employer thinks, *She is involved with someone who is not reputable, who is dodgy and dishonest.* It puts a huge question mark over you, regardless of what has happened. He was creating a drama. I said to the man at this company, "Don't worry, it's this guy I'm having trouble with." But once they found out I had any association with him, I felt I had to give up some of my projects and my work. The waters had become so murky. I didn't want my clients harassed and I didn't want prospective clients to know about it. When you have a stalker, you become a liability, and no one wants to work with a liability. Essentially the stalker won – he was successful in his attempt to hurt me.

'It's very tricky when you are being harassed online and through other people. First, it's hard to justify it without sounding as if you are trying to cover something up and, secondly, you don't have access to the conversation or the email the third party has received. When the 50 people who contacted me said they had received this email, I wasn't in a position to say, flick it to me – let me see it. I didn't know what was being said about me. So I had to justify myself without having seen exactly what I was being accused of.

'You bring people into your life in a trusting way,' Barbara says, 'and they get you into a psychological bind. There is just nothing you can do. My world was falling apart, everything I had worked for and the credibility I felt I was building up was being destroyed. He had found my weak spot, what is most important to me, which is my work, and he exploited that. He was spending a ridiculous amount of time trying to do this. I think he was angry.' Barbara felt helpless. 'I am quite good at damage control,' she says, 'but you simply can't argue with crazy – there was no logical answer or course of action I could have taken to change his behaviour. It was out of my hands.'

Barbara's online presence was how she got most of her work. She had to close that down for a while. 'You don't realise how many footprints you leave online. You pretty much draw a map for a stalker every single day and then you update it. I was inadvertently hand-delivering him information of who I was with, what I was doing at a particular time, what I was planning to do and what I enjoyed doing last week. I was drawing him a map to my life and there was no way to delete it or remove myself and stop feeding him information. I had to protect my tweets, change my Facebook settings so it would remain private. I had to be careful about specifics otherwise anyone I mentioned would get emails from him. It temporarily derailed the way I was trying to develop my whole career.'

Apart from Eva, whom 'he was spending hours a day contacting people about and harassing at the same time,' Barbara felt she couldn't talk to anyone about the stalking. 'You don't know how they will react, even good friends. It's hard to explain that this is a new breed of business or career stalkers. Both my parents are psychologists and I can tell Mum all my problems, but I can't tell her about this – she would think putting information online was ridiculous. I told a couple of girlfriends about it but I didn't really have a lot of support from them. If you tell men in your life, the first thing they want to do is grab a baseball bat and head over there. You can't contain it as much when you start to involve other people – everyone has an opinion. People close to me want to fight the battle for me or will offer up silly advice. It exacerbates the problem and suddenly you have to deal with the opinions of 20 people.'

The grey areas associated with cyberstalking were emphasised when Barbara reported the behaviour to the police. 'It wasn't as if my life was threatened, it wasn't as though he was sending me love letters or saying he was going to physically hurt me. It wasn't like that. But it was what I considered equally as damaging and equally as sinister – taking away my livelihood and destroying my credibility, which I had worked for. I just can't get that back. I would actually have preferred that he ransacked my house than destroyed my career because my professional reputation and career are so valuable to me. Particularly in the career I am in, it's all about the people and what they say about you.'

As lawyer Vic Rajah says, 'Barbara's story illustrates the perils of the internet and of online perpetrators who carefully select their prey, ingratiate themselves with the target and inflict wanton damage if their warped perceptions and motives are damaged. Restraining orders exist but unless there is regular communications targeted at the victim it is very difficult to establish stalking.' And as Barbara points out, 'The internet has been widely used for several decades and the advice I was given was to rely on a block button or to defriend them. But to defriend a stalker or block him online is just not that simple. The law was my last option. It's horrific how stalkers can actually use the law – and often are the first to access it. The weird thing was that when I told people about being stalked, they were asking if I had signed any agreements with him, have I checked all the emails I have sent him, have I said anything to upset him that he can legally go me for?'

It seemed to Barbara that she would have been treated more seriously by the law if she had been bleeding or her life had been threatened physically. But, as she says, 'this person is ruining my livelihood and career and and that is as bad. This is my happiness, my mental health and my well-being. Stalking is not always, "I'm going to come and kill you if you won't be mine", like in the movies. It can be something as simple as, "Don't hire this woman." That is abuse, that is stalking. But if it isn't something violent in nature, a threat to my property or to me physically, then there was nothing the police could really do. There is no law against being an asshole, a dangerous asshole.'

In order to work out the best way of handling the situation, Barbara read a lot about stalking, including 'an interesting article online by a woman who said "buy a gun". That's really bad. In the early stages I wanted to tackle it head on and write him this giant email and really break everything down and tell him he can't treat me this way. But the common idea was not to contact the stalker because it feeds the fire, so I decided not to – because you can't argue with crazy. Hopefully he knows what he is doing is out of bounds and insane, but I thought there is no point igniting the fire.

'What is interesting is that people sometimes keep the stalking a secret. Ideally I would have copied and pasted his inflammatory emails and messages and said, "Look at what

I was sent – isn't this crazy?" It is crazy and it is hard and exhausting. But if the stalker hasn't already contacted some of your professional contacts, then you are revealing everything that has been said about you. I had a long, serious think about different ways to approach it. There is no easy answer because you are dealing with someone who is not logical.'

What Barbara did decide to do was to write to all her friends and professional contacts. 'I wrote them a short email that said, "This man has become dangerous to me. Please don't be in contact with him, please ignore him if he writes you an email." It's not the best conversation to have, especially if you think it's not going to be effective. It also creates more questions or people kind of shrug you off or ask, "What did you do to upset him?" Some of them say, "I'm not taking sides", and I'm thinking, *It's not really about taking sides – they think where there is smoke there is fire.*'

Because one of the main ways the stalker pursued Barbara was through a sustained campaign against her in emails and texts to third parties, the harassment is unstoppable: 'He will say something to a third party with the idea they will tell people who will tell more people. There is just no way I can defend myself to all these people.' Barbara never knew who was hearing the whispers about her or the amount of damage it has caused. She also had very little evidence – 'I have got a couple of text messages that I have saved but nothing really concrete' – because much of the stalking has been done by involving other people. 'There is no blood-stained letter, no crime, because he has done it in a way that is almost untraceable. When I talk about it, I feel like I am talking about a ghost – and they make you feel that you are mad, paranoid.'

What makes stalking so poisonous is that there is no way you can measure or explain it, indeed there is no start or end point and no way to contain it. Barbara eventually wrote an article about the stalking of women in the media. 'When they come out about being bullied, people say, "Suck it up, princess, it's part of the job. Grow some balls." How dare they? No one should have to become immune to mistreatment – that is just insane. There is this perception that when a media woman is being bullied, she must have written something controversial and pushed buttons. People think you provoke stalking and provoke bullying – they think it takes two to tango. It could be perceived as there is a stranger talking rubbish about me or alternatively this is a business relationship that has gone wrong.'

Barbara has become really anxious. 'I am always on edge walking home in the dark, even though I don't believe this guy is violent – he is quite a small man and has never threatened physical violence. But being tormented like this has made me feel physically scared. I lock all the doors and I hate sleeping in the house when other people aren't home.' And the stalking has changed how she is with people. 'You become really careful,' she says. 'I have developed what I call an inner circle – I have to know someone for years before they will be admitted. It's even ruined my romantic relationships. I'm not interested in dating. I'm scared about what people will try to get out of me or how they are going to affect my career or what they are going to say about me.

'I'm in my 20s and I want to be able to go out and talk to people. I want to open myself up to new relationships. I want to be making friends. I want to have lots of plans on the weekend. But because of this whole stalking thing, it's like I am cynical beyond my years. I feel worn down, I feel distrusting, I feel angry and I feel pissed off at how things as simple as connecting with a person on Twitter can turn into something that is just so brutal. You have to be very careful who you invite into your world. That is not what I imagined before this began – it was the more people I can connect with, the more people I can bring into my world and the more places I can go. I want to have dates most nights of the week, I don't want to turn down invitations. I want to do all that stuff.

'But when I meet someone new I'm wondering whether they could be a liability to my happiness. They are not a potential business colleague, friend or boyfriend – they are just someone who can ruin me. That is quite a sad effect of what has happened. Although I suppose it is better that it has happened early on rather than in the middle of my career.'

Barbara finds that people's perceptions of the stereotypical stalker complicate their reactions. 'They think it has got to be romantic, someone you have slept with, and perhaps it is going to be about physical violence. They think stalking only happens to high-profile people, and they feel that it's a real ego thing – they think you are exaggerating, you think your profile is bigger than it is – because only famous people have stalkers.'

There is also a perception that 'you're the idiot for putting stuff out on social media. But that's catch 22 because in my field you need to be online to make contacts and interact with people. Yes, you are giving people a certain amount of personal information but you are not giving them free rein to do what they want with it. You have to be really careful. I could have written something that is equally as damaging to him and called him out for being a serial pest. But if I did that, I could actually implode. There is just so much shame attached to it. People reading it could react in all sorts of ways and I could ruin my own career.'

Barbara moved house, not wholly because of what happened, but she thought it was a good opportunity to preserve her privacy. She has not told anyone where she lives. 'I have been trying to think of ways to be private. I need to be public for work though and have to give people my email address and phone numbers and put them on my website. It is so hard to promote yourself and your business on the internet without giving the stalker information. You have to be out there. If you start hiding, then you have lost. I don't want my career to be affected by this. I don't want to worry about every decision I make – whether I can walk home at 9pm or post a tweet or call this person or give my phone number out to this man I met.'

'The stalker in this case is targeting a particular type of person who he believes he will be able to influence and who will look up to him,' says psychologist Gary Rubin, 'and that profile seems to fit Barbara – young, career-driven and potentially impressionable. Things start out well, given he knows the approach to take to entice his victim, but when things don't go to plan and he starts feeling a loss of control, he becomes unhinged and tries to restore order/control by re-engaging Barbara.' Then, as she continues to withdraw, his loss of control is exacerbated, causing him to act with reckless abandon to the point of harassing the victim via all her connections. The stalker usually has an idealised fantasy of whatever his agenda or goal is and is very determined to achieve it. It's like, *If I cannot have you, I will have to destroy you.*

Barbara would have been drawn to the stalker because potentially he offered something that aligned with her goals – in this case, networking and career development. Using Eva, another woman of the same age and similar type, was a clever way of Barbara being deceived into thinking, *If this is working for someone who is similar to me, then perhaps this will be positive for me too.* As Gary Rubin says, Barbara's description of how the perpetrator started acting as if he was the victim is not uncommon because often a stalker is genuinely convinced that 'they are the one who has been wrong done by and, through this sense of entitlement, must seek justice. The victim is then put in a difficult position, as Barbara described, where she feels no choice but to defend the allegations made against her in order to protect her credibility.'

Chapter 7
Physically Threatened

An entire generation of Australians grew up watching Lorraine Bayly on television, in *The Sullivans*, *Carson's Law*, *Neighbours* and *Play School*, as well as in films such as *The Man from Snowy River* and on stage. Some were watching with sinister intentions. Lorraine has been stalked by several fans, one of whom physically threatened her.

She had to move house three times after stalking episodes. 'I was doing a lot of television work in Melbourne and people found out where I was living,' Lorraine says. 'The first time it was people knocking at the door constantly and one of them was a little bit scary. I put up with it for a while but in the end I had to move. Then it happened a second time, the same kind of thing but with different people who would stay outside my house. It was uncomfortable to start with. But then it escalated when a man tried to ram down my front door – thankfully it was a very heavy door, but it was quite frightening.'

When Lorraine was forced to move the third time, she had bars put on every window and security doors installed. 'I did feel safer,' she says. But despite these measures, she was harassed again. 'Three men banged on the front door and called out my name. They were banging really hard. I was terrified. When the police arrived, the men split up and scampered off in three different directions, which meant it was impossible to catch them.'

These stalking events affected Lorraine so much that she felt unsafe in her own home. But there was another incident that was more frightening and dangerous. She was at a social event outside the city, where a man 'was acting very suspiciously and was asking people about me. I was lucky that they became concerned and alerted the police, who tracked him down. At the time of his arrest he was carrying a bag. When I asked what was in the bag, the policeman said, "You don't want to know", inferring that whatever it was could have caused me a great deal of harm.'

Since then Lorraine has enhanced the security at her home and she doesn't tell people where she lives. 'Something like that makes you realise how vulnerable you are.' She has also taken self-defence classes and says that she feels safer now.

Some people believe that what happens on television is real and, as psychologist Gary Rubin explains, feel such a strong connection with a character that they lose perspective. 'They forget that it is fiction and that an actor is playing a role. This can be problematic because the person may have negative feelings about the character which are related to something they associate with their own life.' For instance, Lorraine played a strong-minded lawyer on television and it may be that the stalker had a terrible marriage or relationship breakdown and held intense resentment and rage towards their former (female) partner, or perhaps they had a bad experience with the law and were opposed by a female lawyer. On the other hand, stalkers who feel a positive connection with a character may become infatuated with the actor playing the part and then expect what they see as positive gestures, such as gift giving and visits, to be accepted with gratitude and responded to in kind. When this does not happen, the stalker takes it as extreme rejection and may want to hurt or destroy the actor.

As Lorraine says, 'You are continually surprised that some people assume these characters are real people. I once played a very nice, sensible, warm, caring character and was asked by a newspaper if I would write an agony-aunt column in the same persona. I said, "No, I am not that character. I will stick to acting, thanks." There are less dangerous things like quite funny letters asking me the best way to treat a child in a particular situation or how to cook something. I don't have children and I don't really enjoy cooking, so I'd be the last person I'd go to for that kind of advice.'

She has also received some very frightening letters.

Lorraine's experience is typical of the type of stalking traumas that celebrities experience. Entertainer Wendy Stapleton has also 'been stalked for four or five years by someone I don't know, have never seen or communicated with. I have no idea where they live or what they do. What I do know is that they know where I live and somehow they have managed to gain access to private information about me. They are trying to bully a member of my family through me, through wearing me down. Whoever this person is, he (or she) is a coward who hides by sending anonymous letters. After all these years I have now been able to ignore them, although they keep coming. Knock yourself out trying,' she says, 'but you're not going to get anywhere through me.'

All stalkers can be dangerous, even when they feel positively connected to someone, because when their advances are rejected they may become violent and threatening. And the person being stalked may not be the only one in danger. People surrounding you – for example, family and friends – may also be in danger. As Gary Rubin comments, 'The impact on Lorraine and others in her industry is very clear. It creates a sense of vulnerability and a lack of safety – so much so that Lorraine even took up martial arts training to protect herself.'

Chapter 8

Suffering from Childhood

Josey grew up in a happy home. Her parents divorced when she was very young, but that never affected her because she had loads of love from both sides. On her mother's side she was an only child and was spoilt with love and when she went to her dad's house she had six siblings, who also loved and cared for her. So she had a supportive, caring and nurturing environment. But her family saw her change from a vibrant young child to a withdrawn teenager.

'It started in Grade 5,' Josey says. 'There was a new girl in the school named Angelina – I was hoping she would be in my class because I had never had any real connections with anyone in my school. I did have friends and a group I would hang around with, but I didn't have a best friend. As it turns out, she was in my class but it didn't turn out the way I had imagined. It turned out that this was going to be the day that I started on my route to becoming a tortured teenager and eventually ending up infested with hatred for the world and everyone in it.

'As soon as she walked in and looked at me the way she

did I knew she was not going to be a friend of mine. She immediately sat next to a girl called Madeleine. Madeleine was the most popular girl in the school – she was pretty, she was kind and she happened to be the one girl who would always ask me to come and sit with her at lunchtime. We had partner-sharing that morning and usually Madeleine would choose me to partner her but that day she chose the new girl, Angelina. I didn't think much of their blooming friendship until lunchtime came and I went and sat with Madeleine, Angelina and some others, Peter, Luke and Jenny. Angelina turned to me as I opened my lunchbox and yelled at the top of her lungs, 'Ewww, she has the grossest looking lunch I've ever seen, kind of like her face.' Everyone laughed and agreed. They asked me to sit somewhere else because they just couldn't look at it or smell it. I don't know why I still remember her exact words, and it was so petty and unimportant compared with what was to follow. But I'll just never forget them.

'The next day was when I realised that I was no longer a part of that group, that now I was alone. I would spend the rest of my school years being tormented by them. It wasn't like it was once in a while that they would throw remarks, objects and hatred my way, it was every single day.'

Angelina soon assumed the role of the ring leader, commencing regular and vicious attacks on Josey. 'The first time Angelina physically taunted me, she tripped me over by running up behind me and kicking the back of my feet while I was walking. I landed flat on my face. I had a scratch on my face and it bled quite a lot. After that day she would hurl nasty comments about how clumsy and stupid I was.

'The last day of Year 6 was supposed to be an exciting

time and by this stage I had some other friends, but they were the types of friends who were school-based only. It was a fun day, until the bell rang to go home. I hadn't heard from any of the bullies that day. And I was going to a different secondary school – my parents made sure of that – and I was so excited to start a new life. I walked my usual way to the gates.

'As I approached the gates, Angelina, Madeleine and Luke were standing there with huge smiles on their faces. I knew it was because they were about to give me one last push, shove or kick. When I left the school grounds I looked awful. I was covered in fish sauce, eggs – anything that stinks had been thrown or attached to me, including a dirty used menstrual pad that was stuck to my back.

'I remember feeling humiliated. I wanted to die. I just wanted it to stop. I hated them, I hated the fact that I had never retaliated. I had never given them a reason to bully me or to prey on me, but it was at that moment that I began to think, *Maybe my lunch did stink, maybe I was ugly and maybe everyone did hate me.* To make matters worse, my mum called me at about 5 o'clock that afternoon and told me my grandfather had died. I'll never forget how I felt that day. It was the worst day of my teenage life.

'I remember asking my mum if I could get foils in my hair and start wearing make-up for high school. I spent the entire school holidays practising doing my hair and getting my make-up just right.

'In the car on the way to school on the first day of Year 7, I had this feeling of dread and reluctance. I was so scared that it was just going to be the same as primary school. It wasn't. The first few months were great. I made new friends, one of whom is still today always by my side, and I was beginning to forget about the people who had made my life hell.'

Like most young people, Josey was soon exposed to social media. So many of her peers were using it and she wanted to fit in. Soon it started to become an important part of her teenage life. Unfortunately, though, Josey trustingly let the bullies back into her life via social media and they recommenced the stalking, escalating it to a whole new level.

'It was the worst mistake of my life,' Josey says. 'Social media is all about how many friends you have and how many likes you have on your selfies would make or break you in high school. So naturally, being 13 years old at the time, I accepted whoever was willing to send me a friend request. I still don't know why I just didn't delete them or block them straight away. Angelina had sent me a request, which I wasn't stupid enough to accept. At this time anyone could send you a private message. She wrote about how sorry she was for her behaviour and all the rest, so I accepted her request.

'Then only hours later I discovered a post on my wall about how pathetic, ugly, stupid, weird and creepy I was. I hadn't realised it was on there. There were so many comments from Peter, Luke, Madeleine and Jenny backing up her claims and lies about me. They had not only stalked me through primary school but also now they were doing it through social media. They wrote that I had given oral sex to a teacher, which was a complete lie. They wrote that I had gone to a party and got so drunk that I had been found naked in a drain, which was also a lie. In everything they had written, there was not one single bit of truth. But no one wanted to know the truth. Everyone at my new school began to whisper as I walked past.

The posts didn't stop and I tried defending their claims, which was another mistake. I wish I had just blocked them.

'After about a month I felt completely drained. I just didn't want to defend myself any more so I deleted Facebook. I didn't want to go to school because I felt I was a laughing stock. But my best friend convinced me to keep coming, to be strong and not let them affect me any more.

'I came out of school one day and to my shock there they were – all five of them, plus a few new faces that I hadn't seen before. I couldn't believe that, because I had deleted Facebook, they were now going to this extreme length to destroy me. My best friend and I turned around and walked off and they shouted out threats. We decided not to retaliate. I felt a kick to the back of my foot and I tripped and fell. There she was, standing over me and shouting. By this stage a crowd had gathered around us. My best friend was standing in shock, she didn't even want to move, and Madeleine pushed her to the ground as well. They stood over us, spitting down on us and saying, "This is what happens to sluts." Both of us were virgins but they couldn't go back on their lies now.

'My best friend didn't come to school that Monday and she didn't answer my texts or my calls. Her mother had suddenly passed away on the Saturday morning and she was not coping. She didn't come back to school for nearly a month. When she returned she looked different. She looked how I felt – skinny, withdrawn and very sad. She showed me how she had dealt with the pain of losing her mum and said that it felt so much better to release the pain. She had been cutting herself.

'That night I received a text – and this was the text that triggered my experience with cutting. Madeleine had got my number through someone at my school and she had started sending me anonymous texts with emojis of guns and knives. When I discovered it was her, I asked her to stop. I felt so desperate at that moment that I let everything out – how I felt, how I wished I was dead, how I couldn't sleep. That just became more ammunition for them. They started texting me things like "Go kill yourself, no one will ever love you, you're so ugly."

'It tipped me over the edge and I began to cut. At the time I was so disconnected that the cutting felt like I was having a dose of heroin. I felt like I was releasing every nasty comment, every physical attack. In my distorted world of distress it felt good. Before I knew it, my arms were completely covered in cuts, blood and scabs. I was hospitalised a few times because of how deep I was cutting.

'My best friend and I decided that cutting was no longer enough. We needed other things to do, to keep our minds off how bad our lives were. We started with weed and soon enough we were trying things like acid and ice. We were becoming everything they were saying we were. If I only knew then what I know now. We were letting them win.'

Josey's situation became even more disturbing for her parents and for those who loved her when she turned to regular drug taking and became even more disconnected. 'The drug use became a massive problem, driving me to suicide attempts. I became isolated because I could not allow myself to be exposed to these people. I didn't want them to find me. Every time they would text I would call the phone company and get my number changed.'

The targeting and stalking continued and so did Josey's

cutting and drug abuse. 'They would wait outside the shopping centre for me. They would draw cuts all over their arms and post it on social media saying they were me. They would call all times of the night. They would find out what parties I would be at and make sure they made an appearance.

'They were cruel and they never stopped. They put so much effort into pursuing me there was nowhere for me to hide.

'One of the last times I saw any of them was when I had left school at the start of Year 10. By this stage I was only smoking weed as I had been in psychiatric wards and detox programs. I remember this day like it was yesterday. I was at the main shopping centre and was with my best friend in the food court eating lunch. There they were, ordering their lunch. I remember this feeling of complete darkness coming over me as if I had seen the devil – and to me they were the devil. These were the people who had ruined my life, the people that had caused me 90 per cent of the heartache I had felt in my life. I felt the need to hide, to make sure I wasn't spotted. But sure enough they spotted me. Angelina had this look on her face that I will never forget – she was half-smiling but not enough for me to notice. They walked straight up to me in the middle of the food court and hurled nasty comments and jokes my way – not only to me but also to my best friend, saying that her mother had killed herself because of her and other horrifying taunts. That's how cruel they were. We sat there until they had enough, until they decided to leave. That night we got so messed up. We cut, we smoked, we did drugs and I nearly lost my best friend to an overdose.

'Years later, I have conquered the drug abuse and cutting with the help of counselling, detox and changing how I view the world. I still see the stalkers every now and then but they ignore me as much as I ignore them.

'My message to any young person in this situation is don't suffer in silence. You are not alone. Seek help before you get into a situation like I did with self-harming and drugs – it's never the answer and you lose years off your life trying to recover.'

Why would children like Angelina and Madeleine bully others and cause them such pain? As children and young adults, we are often so insecure and unsure about ourselves we are strangely comforted observing – or imagining – differences in others. Former MP Tammy Lobato suffered from alopecia. 'Having no hair and wearing bad wigs meant I was a target for those seeking to increase their self-esteem by virtue of others' differences. My alopecia brought out the best and worst in others and received the most attention and reactions in secondary school. In response I learned to be tough, to stand up for myself and to become a leader. My advice to young people with hair loss or other conditions is to be proactive, open and informative about their situation – to give others the greatest chance at feeling compassion. The less secretive the information, the less attractive is the impulse to bully. The other advice I share is that with maturity comes greater acceptance of difference and even empathy and understanding. As adults and parents, it is important to continue the culture change required to protect and respect all others.'

As a community if we start to stamp out bullying and stalking at a young age perhaps we can all help in some small way to protect young people like Josey from suffering the effects from many years of trauma. Eric Castillo, who works for one of Australia's leading banks, says, 'Treat people the way you would like to be treated yourself.' As Banyule City Councillor Peter Castaldo says, 'We've all seen bullying in several forms throughout our lives, from school to the workplace and in the home. Whether it's physical or psychological, it's up to us to stand up to bullying as soon as it arises.'

'Bullying saps potential and creativity and limits experience,' says MP Danielle Green. 'At home, school or work, on the streets or sporting field, it almost always has its roots in childhood. Early intervention must be the key to curing this pervasive problem. Thankfully there's now community conversations and many calls for action.'

Chapter 9

Dangerously Jealous

'When you have a stalker in your life, you're never calm,' Helen says. 'You know that you're suffering from anxiety, you feel so low, you're depressed, you're thinking the worst.' Helen became friends with a man called Greg when he began working in the same company. A group of people from the office would go out socially. The first time Greg was included, he told Helen that he didn't have a girlfriend. She offered to set him up with one of her friends. 'From day one I had no interest in him and I made that clear. We were friends, we had a friendship for about three years.' Helen liked to go for walks at lunchtimes and Greg would go with her. 'Then when I started seeing someone in our group, I told him about it. He pulled me aside. "I would do anything for you," he said.' Helen's mother interpreted that as a declaration of love. 'But I didn't think anything of it,' Helen says.

From that point on, Greg pursued Helen. On one occasion he brought her 12 long-stemmed roses. When she asked him what they were for, he said, 'It's all in the card.' The card said 'I love you'. 'That's really sweet but we're mates and that's all we're ever going to be,' Helen said. 'Normally, when I have come across men who liked me that way but who I wasn't interested in,' she says, 'I'd just tell them and they'd either deal with it or the friendship would end. But this wasn't like that.'

After about nine months, her relationship with her colleague broke up. A few weeks later she started to go out with someone else. When she told Greg, 'he became very weird. I couldn't deal with the way he was acting. He was angry with me and annoyed. He began picking on all my faults and telling me things he didn't like about me – such as how I would make him late when we were going for a walk – something he had never done before. One time I did some singing at an open-mike night and Greg was making remarks about how bad my performance was, saying really nasty things about me. That night at the bar, he stood two metres away from me and the guy I was with and gave us really dirty looks.

'I spoke to him the next day and asked what was wrong. I spent about an hour trying to get to the bottom of it. But it gets to the point when you just get over it and you can't deal with it any more. He just kept saying, "I want to speak to you. I want to meet up with you. Just let me buy you a coffee." He sent one message that said something like, it's been this number of weeks, this number of days and this number of minutes since we last spoke. Can I just buy you a cup of coffee or do you just not want to be friends any more? I'd never ever kissed this guy. I was so over the friendship and his weirdness. I replied that I didn't want to be friends.'

Greg began inundating Helen with text messages, phone calls and voice messages. He made several websites about her. One of these was saying 'sorry' and included a letter that needed an email address to access, so he could monitor if Helen had opened and read it. She ignored it.

He would intercept her on her way to work. Helen knew that this wasn't his normal route to work and that he was going that way in order to see her. At one point he threw his arm out in front of her. 'I remember coming in from a lunchbreak, shaking because I had seen him. Looking back, I shouldn't have been like that, but the situation makes you feel so stressed, scared and alone and you make bad choices. I couldn't deal with it, so my mother, who he knew, went to talk to him. She said, "My daughter is not interested in you. Just move on – don't call her, don't text her any more. She is just not interested in you."

'The calls and texts stopped for a while. But after a time he resumed his stalking behaviour. Not every day, but he knew my routine, where I walked on my lunch breaks. He sent a letter to my office with the address typed so I wouldn't know it was from him. I ripped open the envelope and inside I could see paper with cut-out letters. I was too frightened to even look at what it said. By this stage I was scared for my life. He had been creating more websites and wrote a daily blog about me, which went on for quite a long time. I was terrified. My brother-in-law called Greg and said, "Just take the websites down. You don't want Helen to go to the police. One day you'll find another girl".'

Greg became very nasty.

About nine months later Helen finally reported him to the police. 'I felt that I tried everything else I could and that he was trying to ruin my life. It had just kept escalating and was getting worse – everything he was doing was becoming worse. The police were really understanding. They couldn't believe

I had waited so long because I had so much evidence of his stalking. The police didn't treat him badly and when they asked him, "Did you do this and do this?", he said, "Yes, yes, yes". They warned him that I could get a restraining order against him. So then he went off and did something even worse and got interviewed again. The police were astounded.'

At the time of writing, about three years after the stalking behaviour began, Helen was on her third restraining order. Without the order she would feel much less safe, she says, although Greg had told her that 'the orders are as useless as tits on a bull'. Even with an order against him, he would still be waiting outside her office. 'I will never feel 100 per cent safe. If he stops doing things for a period, I feel a little bit better, but I never feel totally safe. I got a prank call recently from a blocked number at 3 o'clock in the morning and so of course I thought it's from him. It may have just been a random prank call but you become paranoid.'

At one point the police detained him because they feared for Helen's safety. 'This was the worst time. Over a two-week period he was contacting me every couple of minutes – I had to collect the evidence for the police and I have a book of screenshots that's 5 centimetres thick. He was writing weird things on his blog and websites. By then he knew not to use my name but he was saying things like, "I see you coming down the windy steps. There is a light above your head", which is a description of where I work. He was writing about killing me. And I was afraid he was going to kill himself because he was saying he was really depressed and that no one would help him. I was terrified he was going to kill himself, or kill me and then himself.'

One of the complications of being stalked is you don't know how other people will react to it. At the beginning, Helen's mother had difficulty believing Greg was stalking her daughter, but she understood after talking to him. 'I didn't tell anyone from work for the first nine months,' Helen says. 'No one had any idea what was happening. I felt very alone – I thought if I told anyone, the story would get around. I guess I felt ashamed. As well as my family, some of my close friends were aware of the stalking. But I didn't tell my partner's parents, who are not at all judgemental – it's just that I didn't want them to know I have to go to court, which is not a nice thing to have in your life. I know someone who'd had a similar problem with her ex-husband and people thought she must have contributed to his behaviour. Some people think, *Why would someone normal have a stalker? There's obviously got to be something wrong with her.* I was terrified and I was embarrassed. I remember thinking no one can know. It wasn't until the police came to my office to see me and I had to go to court that I told my employer.'

When Helen finally did tell her friends and colleagues, 'Some people made jokes about it, which is not what you want to hear. It's not a joke. Others would suggest getting someone to break his kneecaps – but I would never want to do that to anyone. My aunty said, "He is not going to kill you – he can't live without you". I couldn't handle people giving me advice or hearing their opinions about his behaviour.'

Helen's life has changed dramatically since the stalking began. 'I don't feel safe. I won't go and hang out the washing after dark, for instance. I'm not friendly to people any more. I used to walk along the street and smile, but now I don't acknowledge people I meet – even if they're 80, I don't feel I can smile at them because that's letting them in. Sometimes I know I'm rude and quite evasive – I don't like being like that but I feel I have to for my own safety.'

At the time of writing, the stalking was continuing. 'I don't expect this problem to go away any time soon,' Helen says. 'My life revolves around it. If it's really bad, I will be scared 24 hours a day. I'm not able to sleep properly. It terrifies me that I might google my name and click on something that's really horrible. I don't know what's out there but it has dramatically changed my life because I know he's out to get me. Unfortunately, he is going to be around for a long time. As soon as one restraining order ends, he starts his websites up again.

'Sometimes I have to go to get a court date organised four times in a month and that's embarrassing because I need to take time off work. I don't have a choice, I have to do it. The worst thing is not knowing what's going to happen in court – whether he's going to have a lawyer with him or go berserk. You feel so messed up, it's scary. My partner has been really good but it stresses him out and he gets upset. We have been together over two-and-a-half years and lived this nightmare together – he has never known anything different.'

Helen says she saw no warning signs that this was going to happen. 'Greg is very smartly dressed. Nothing about him would have made me think he would ever do anything like this. All I did was be polite and friendly to this man I met at work because he didn't have many friends. Now he has changed my life forever. It's really weird, with everything he has done to me – and he's done horrible things to me – I still remember when I knew him before the stalking began and he seemed to be a person with a good heart.

'It's almost like he's doing this so he can remain a part of my life – it's like this big sick game in which he gets to see me in court and I have no choice but to be involved with him.'

Chapter 10
The Big Mistake

A successful businessman with a close network of much-loved family and friends, Peter took on the role of night-time manager at one of his brother's video shops to distract himself when he separated from his wife. One of the regular customers was a woman named Christine, who was friendly and Peter found pleasant to talk with. After a while she was visiting the video store frequently and it got to the point where she would just 'hang around' and talk to Peter, sometimes until closing time at midnight. This went on for several months until one day she simply came out and said, 'Why have you never asked me out?' Peter said that it had never entered his mind. 'Well, I think you should take me out,' she said.

Peter agreed. It was a 'big mistake. Not that I knew it at the time. We went out for about four or five months. I never allowed my social life to come between me and my children, who were nine and five at the time. Christine met them the first time at a "surprise" encounter. When she was with them she would say things like, "I really love your father. Would you like to have a little brother or sister?" Years later my daughter told me that Christine had said to her, "I want to have your father's children".'

She convinced Peter to give her a key to his apartment and she began to bring more and more of her belongings around, as if in preparation for moving in permanently. 'It was during this period that she started to become "strange",' Peter says. 'I often had evening appointments and wouldn't get home until rather late. She was always there waiting for me with questions about who I had seen, where I'd been. In the beginning, I took all this as fun, nothing serious. However, I found out later that she would ask the staff at the video shop if they knew where I was, who I was with.'

Peter never regarded his friendship with Christine as a relationship and told her this on many occasions. She would reply that he would change his mind one day.

When his father was diagnosed with cancer, Peter began to spend more and more time with him. During this period he didn't see much of Christine but she would be always 'available' just in case he needed her.

After his father died, Peter decided to move back to his family home, which was now empty. 'I didn't see Christine at all for some time because I didn't tell her my new address. Then one day I received a phone call from her. She began by saying that because of my recent loss she had decided to give me some space to get over it, but that now would be a good time for us to get together again. I tried to explain that we never had a relationship and I had told her this many times – so there was no point in us "getting together" again.'

At that, Christine seemed to change tack. She said that she understood that and only wanted to go out for dinner every now and then, with no strings attached. What was he doing the following night, she asked. When Peter said he was meeting some friends, she suggested they go out another time.

'I went out the next night with a female friend, who came to pick me up and then dropped me off back at home,' Peter says. 'I had been inside the house no more than two minutes when the phone rang. "Good-looking mates you have. You didn't say you were going out with another woman," Christine shouts. "I give you some space to get over your father and you go out with other women."

'I immediately thought, *How does she know where I live and that I'm home?* I went out the front, keeping in the shadows, and looked up and down the street. Sure enough, it was dark but I could just barely make out her car. Enough is enough, I told her, she had no right to interfere in my life. I can go out with whosoever I liked. She let go of all sorts of expletives and then hung up the phone.'

About a week later there was a knock on Peter's door. Christine was crying and very apologetic, insisting that she didn't know why she'd acted that way. 'She was standing on my porch crying with people walking past, which was awkward, so I asked her to come in.' After a while she calmed down, but only because she was getting ready for another attack, a barrage of questions about why Peter had broken off with her and how they could get back together. In order to avoid a meltdown, Peter calmed her down by saying that he would consider it, but needed time because of what had happened. Christine was happy with that and left.

Peter never intended to contact her, take any of her calls or open the door to her again.

She had other ideas. 'I would see her car parked down the street or up around the corner at least two or three times a week,' Peter says. 'She was still harassing the staff at the video shop and, as a joke, they would say, "Someone with a dead rabbit was asking for you", alluding to the scene in the film *Fatal Attraction*.'

This went on for about another three or four months until eventually Christine just disappeared.

About three years after this happened and Peter had had no further contact with Christine, he was making a call to a client, which was answered by a receptionist. When she heard who was calling, she shrieked. 'Is that you Peter? It's me, Christine.' Fortunately for Peter, nothing came of it. The last anyone heard of Christine, she was married, had children and was living in a town an hour's drive away from Peter.

Part III

Chapter 11

If You Are Being Stalked

If you are being stalked and you feel your life is in danger or you are emotionally distressed, you should immediately seek professional assistance.

The following is information that might assist you, depending on the circumstances.

- If you know who the stalker is, you can apply to the court for a restraining order.
- Report any intimidation or stalking behaviour, property damage or assault to police.
- If assaulted, obtain medical attention and take photographs of damage or injuries as a permanent record. This evidence may be used in any legal proceedings.
- Keep a diary of any significant event, including dates and times of any phone calls received and, if possible, record the caller for evidence. Save voice messages on an answering machine or phone.
- Keep any gifts, text messages, emails, letters or cards

received. Handle gifts, letters and cards as little as possible and place in a bag, as forensic evidence may be collected later (eg, fingerprints).

- If a vehicle is continually parked outside your home or workplace, take a photo or video it if possible. Note the registration number, car make and colour.
- Keep a record of the names, addresses and contact numbers of any witnesses to the stalker's actions.
- Keep a record of the names and contact numbers of people you have reported the incident to or sought help from (eg, friends, police, court staff and doctors).

Restraining or intervention orders

This course of action should be carefully considered, after discussions with police, legal experts and victim advocates. It can be a useful deterrent but, on the other hand, may give the target a false sense of security. In addition, it may not deter stalkers, particularly those who have a strong sense of power over the victim, have continued the behaviour for a long time or those with a history of violence. It is important to have a safety plan in place before applying for a restraining order. See Laws Against Stalking (pages 119–126) for more information.

Police will require the facts and proof of any stalking or bullying incidences that you have been subjected to. To support your complaint, have the following information with you when reporting the matter to police:

- The nature of the relationship you have had with the stalker, if any.
- If there is or has been any restraining orders or other

court orders in place involving the stalker, take the order to police so they can make a copy for their file.

- Your diary and/or notes recording the dates and times of all sightings, telephone conversations, including taped conversations and videos; and names and addresses of witnesses. If you have one, include a photo of the stalker.
- Your mobile phone so you can show the police evidence of text messages, emails and voicemails received from the stalker.

General safety tips

Contact

In no circumstances should you agree to meet the stalker to talk about the stalking. This also applies to responding to texts, emails, letters, phone calls etc. You can ask a friend or your lawyer to contact them if you want to get a message to them.

Routines

Vary routines, including routes to work, shopping centres and other places visited frequently. Try to vary the stores where you frequently shop.

Use of telephones

See Cyberstalking (below).

Post office boxes

Consider having all your mail, including magazine subscriptions, sent to a post office box. This is particularly useful if you live in an apartment complex, preventing the stalker from finding your apartment number. Destroy all mail that you throw away that contains your name and address.

Banks

You may be asked for your mother's maiden name as a security password. This name is available to anyone researching public records. Instead, say you want to use something else.

Real estate agents

If you are renting your home, consider informing the real estate agency of your stalking situation and gain an undertaking from them that they will not give your address to anyone.

Anonymous or silent elector status

If you are registered to vote, your name and address will appear on a publicly available electoral roll for anyone to see. In the United Kingdom, Australia and New Zealand, it is possible to become a silent or anonymous elector – anyone who believes that having their address shown on the publicly available electoral roll could put their personal safety, or their family's safety, at risk can apply. Anonymous elector status is not granted automatically; each application is decided on whether the claims made by the applicant meet the conditions.

Personal alarms

If you fear for your physical safety when you are in a public place, carry a personal alarm in your hand so you can use it immediately to scare off an attacker. Make sure it is designed to continue sounding if it's dropped or falls to the ground. Personal alarms are often available where travel accessories are sold. Do not carry anything that is meant for use as a weapon.

Safe places

When out and about, if you feel anxious, look for places such as 24-hour petrol stations and shops, police stations and other emergency service centres where you could go for help.

Cyberstalking

Cyberstalking, defined by NetAlert, is 'when a person is stalked or harassed by another person using a service of the internet such as email, instant messaging or via a posting in a discussion group. Stalking behaviours can include threats, cryptic messages and sexual innuendo that occur in a frequent and intrusive manner.' This online behaviour has presented various jurisdictional issues for legislatures to address.

Research shows that cyberstalking is simply another technique the stalkers use – they continue to harass people offline, but will use online sources, such as social media sites, to gather information about their victim. Education programs about online safety in schools provide an invaluable tool to help address cyberbullying, which is common among schoolchildren and adolescents.

General cybersafety

As soon as you realise you are uncomfortable with the nature of a person's communications, you should make it very clear that you do not want these behaviours to continue. You may be frightened to do this, but it is important to make it clear that you do not want to have any further contact with the stalker. If it still continues, you will have to take other measures.

- Seek support from family or friends – do not feel that you have to go through this alone or that you are the only one who has experienced cyberstalking.
- Report the behaviour to the police, with supporting evidence (see above).
- There are also a number of organisations online that can direct people to what to do in their particular circumstance.

Smartphones

Mobile phones provide stalkers with a portable tool to torment their victims, re-dialing numbers, leaving numerous voice messages and sending texts. Malicious calls can also include hang-up calls when you hear the caller put the receiver down followed by the busy tone; or silence, obscene or abusive calls when the caller holds the line open with silence or speaks in an abusive or obscene manner. If you have noticed a pattern of unwelcome calls, keep details of calls (date, time, duration) and contact your phone provider.

The following safety tips are also applicable to landlines.

- Incriminating evidence – text messages, voicemail, emails, photos – may be captured on your SIM card, so do not dispose of it or your mobile phone.
- Get a new phone number and restrict who you give it to. Mobile phone numbers can be changed by contacting

your service provider.

- If you use a landline, get a second phone number. If possible, keep the old number active and connected to an answering machine or voicemail, then use Caller ID or have a friend screen the calls and save any messages from the stalker – these messages, particularly if abusive or threatening, can be used as evidence in a stalking case.

- When you get a new phone number, ask a friend to record a brief outgoing message. For example, a man's voice on a woman's mobile and a simple 'Please leave a message' (with no identifying data) might throw the caller off balance.

- Keep a mobile phone nearby at all times, and ensure you have enough coverage, particularly in regional areas.

Location services

Like social media accounts, global-positioning technology has become a weapon of abuse in the wrong hands, giving abusers an omnipotence they did not possess previously. Hacked social media and email accounts accessing GPS technology on smartphones create new avenues for stalkers.

A recent study found that the technology has created a constantly evolving threat to the safety of women fleeing domestic abuse. The Domestic Violence Resource Centre of Victoria in Melbourne, Australia, surveyed 152 people who work in the domestic violence sector and 46 survivors in response to mounting anecdotal evidence about smartphone harassment. Almost 100 per cent of the workers reported direct experiences of perpetrators using mobile phones to stalk victims, 82 per cent reported smartphones had been used, and about 29 per cent of workers identified GPS or GPS-based tracking applications were being used. Of the survivors, 63 per cent felt they were being watched or tracked.

One domestic violence worker described a family having to flee because the perpetrator located them via the victim's son becoming an online friend with another boy who had his location linked to his name. One woman discovered her husband was monitoring her emails through a forwarding rule he set up after hacking her account and taking control of her phone. Another woman was stalked by her former partner through a GPS-tracking app.

General safety tips
- Turn location services off.
- Set up a secret lock and a PIN on your phone.
- Do not share an Apple/iTunes/iCloud account.

If you suspect you're being tracked
- Return your phone to default settings.
- Disable wi-fi and 3G/4G.
- Take screenshots of anything suspicious (see below).

The internet
Always be conscious about what information about yourself you are placing on social media sites or providing to companies and organisations. The following are suggestions for how to protect yourself when using the internet.

General safety tips

- Never give anyone your password, even if they claim to be from your internet provider, bank or other reputable organisation.
- Do not provide personal information, such as phone number, address, credit card details or photos, to anyone you talk to on social media.
- Be aware that once you post information, including photos, you lose control of what happens to it.
- If you agree to meet someone you have connected with online, take a friend with you and meet them in a public area.
- Leave a chat room immediately if you feel uncomfortable.
- Keep copies of any threatening messages received as evidence.

Social media sites

- Do not use your full name – instead, use a nickname that makes it difficult to trace your real identity.
- Use the 'Block' or 'Ignore' features. They were created so that you can keep out unwanted interactions with other users. They are not fail-safe, but can certainly help.
- Never use easy-to-guess secret questions when setting up online accounts. 'Mother's maiden name' or 'Dog's name' are far too easy for a potential stalker to work out.
- Use a secure password that is a combination of letters, numbers and symbols.
- Change your password often.

- Social media websites have many built-in privacy settings – set as much information as possible to 'private'.
- Only allow your trusted friends and family to view private information.
- Do not add someone as a friend unless you really do know them. A common tactic of stalkers is to create profiles that are not genuine, add their target as a 'friend' and then monitor and stalk them anonymously.

Blogs, tweets and chat rooms
- Be aware of the information you are posting. Small, trivial details in a single post may not be a concern, but over time these details can add up to paint a picture a stalker could use.
- Regularly posting about your movements can also be harmful. A tweet about how you are heading to the beach for the day is letting everyone know your house is empty.

Keep copies of offending material

- Offending emails should be kept on a separate hard disk and a copy printed out. Originals should not be deleted.
- Messages or photographs sent by the stalker to your mobile phone should also be kept. The police can download SIM cards to retrieve these messages.
- Voice messages left by the stalker can also provide valuable evidence and should be saved.

Taking a screenshot

If you receive something suspicious or offensive, capture this evidence by means of a screenshot. A screen capture can be taken in the following ways:

Windows

- Ensure what you want to capture is on screen, then press the 'Print Screen' button on your keyboard. This button is often abbreviated to 'Prnt Scn' or something similar and is usually found in the top righthand corner of the keyboard.
- Click on 'Start'.
- Click 'Programs' or 'All Programs'.
- Click 'Accessories'.
- Double-click on the program 'Paint'.
- When Paint is open, click on 'Edit' in the tool bar, then select 'Paste'.
- You should see the image of your previous screen within the Paint window.
- Save this file on to your desktop. You will now be able to open the picture and it will show everything that was previously on your screen.

Apple

- To take a picture of the whole screen, press the Command + Shift + 4 keys at the same time.
- You can save the file to your desktop.

Supporting someone experiencing stalking

If you know someone who is experiencing stalking, depending on the circumstances you should seek professional advice.

There are several things you can do to support them:

- remain calm
- listen, giving them your full attention
- validate their feelings – eg, 'It's okay to feel scared'
- reassure them it was right for them to tell someone
- ask what you can do to support them
- empower them to seek help.

Chapter 12

Laws Against Stalking

Since the first anti-stalking law was passed, in California in 1990, many countries have criminalised stalking. This has raised awareness about the nature of stalking among the public, the police and the judiciary. Previously, it was not well understood that pursuing someone and being a persistent, unwanted and often threatening presence in their lives was a crime. One of the consequences is that offences involving harassment and threatening behaviour have increased markedly and have become more newsworthy, particularly when they include any form of cyberbullying or cyberstalking. Lawyer and Stop Stalking Now Foundation public officer Mary Boardman says, 'Courts, the legal system and organisations like the Foundation are shining a light on this behaviour. Victims deserve empowerment to have a voice as they bravely step forward'.

But stalking can be a difficult crime to prosecute and often stalkers end up getting charged with lesser offences that are easier to prove, such as breaching a restraining order or using a telephone service to harass. It is good that the person is getting charged for committing a crime, but it does mean that the scope of their behaviour and the overall impact on the target are not really presented in court, and sometimes may not be reflected in sentencing. In addition, some victims of stalking have had nightmarish experiences attempting to get justice because the perpetrators understand the law and how to use it to their own advantage.

One of the difficulties in successfully prosecuting stalkers lies in the nature of stalking and the fact that it is a 'constellation of behaviours', any of which, by itself may seem innocuous. Another is that many anti-stalking laws require proof that a perpetrator had either intent to commit an illegal act and/or to cause fear in the victim, or they require the victim to have felt fear or distress as a result of the stalker's behaviour.

Legislators have attempted to address these problems through the way they have written their laws. But legal definitions of stalking differ between jurisdictions and, likewise, anti-stalking laws in each jurisdiction are different. Some laws define the conduct constituting stalking too narrowly. Some laws require or imply the need for direct physical contact between the perpetrator and the victim, so that electronic monitoring, surveillance or third-party contact (stalking by proxy) initiated by the stalker is not considered stalking.

Constellation of behaviours

Applying the laws appropriately requires police, prosecutors and judges or magistrates who really understand what stalking is. The challenge is always the same: difficulties recognising when stalking is occurring, problems in being able to prove the pattern of behaviour, and having courts that recognise when a pattern of behaviour that might, on the surface, look mild (for example, telephone calls and sending gifts) is actually causing quite severe harm.

Anti-stalking legislation in New Zealand and most Australian states and territories have a prescriptive format, which stipulates the acts that constitute stalking. The main criticisms levelled at prescriptive models is the need to continually amend the law as technology develops and as stalkers devise new and more inventive behaviours that have not been identified in the original legislation. Prohibiting a specific behaviour can simply lead the stalker to employ another form of harassment.

Laws in the UK, many US state jurisdictions and two Australian states do not define stalking in terms of an exhaustive list of possible behaviours. Rather, they define it as a 'course of conduct' or 'series of acts' that constitute harassment or intimidation, without specifying the nature of those acts. This approach is intended to be more inclusive of the victims' experiences of harassment and give the courts the discretion to determine whether a particular 'course of conduct' constitutes stalking. A criticism of this approach is that it creates discrepancies between victim definitions of stalking and those in the minds of police, prosecutors and judges, and that this ambiguity makes it difficult to standardise the definition of stalking and the implementation of the law.

Intent

Many anti-stalking laws require that prosecutors prove that a stalker had an intent to cause fear or distress in the victim. The need to prove intent can be fatal to a stalking case; indeed, many stalkers do not intend to frighten or intimidate their target and others may have a mental illness that prevents them from understanding the harmfulness or unwanted nature of their behaviour. Consequently, many anti-stalking prosecutions have resulted in 'not guilty' findings, even where stalkers have caused great harm to their victims over extended periods of time.

To address this legal difficulty, in Britain and many US jurisdictions, legislation includes both a subjective standard to assess whether the victim experienced emotional distress, and an objective standard of whether a 'reasonable person' would have experienced distress if subjected to the stalker's behaviours. The objective 'reasonable person' test means that it is sufficient to show that the stalker knew or *ought to have known* that their behaviour may cause the target to feel fear or apprehension. This is significant because the court need not take account of the stalker's subjective 'intent' – it is sufficient to show they should have foreseen the consequences of their actions.

In most jurisdictions, the victim's response to the behaviour is a crucial element of establishing the offence. The New Zealand law omits any reference to the victim's subjective response, as well as excluding the requirement that the stalker has intent to cause fear or harm. This approach widens the applicability of the laws so more resilient victims who do not experience, or admit to experiencing, emotional distress are also able to obtain legal recourse.

Threats of violence

The weakest form of anti-stalking legislation requires the

victim to have felt fear or distress as a result of the behaviour. Rather than relying on the 'reasonable person' test, many US anti-stalking laws require that the perpetrator make a credible threat of violence against the victim; others include threats against the victim's immediate family or require that the alleged stalker's course of conduct constitutes an implied threat. For instance, the US federal statute refers to 'conduct that causes, attempts to cause, or would be reasonably expected to cause substantial emotional distress' and 'places [a] person in reasonable fear of ... death ... or serious bodily injury'. These laws are inadequate in addressing behaviours that involve harassment that falls short of threatening violence (and which may be a prelude to violence). Moreover, this victim-response model creates an additional burden of proof and may deny more resilient victims a legal remedy.

Cyberstalking

Cyberstalking – threats made via electronic communication, such as email or the internet – is a criminal offence in many jurisdictions. But there are considerable variations. Some have included prohibitions against harassing electronic, computer or email communications in their harassment legislation; others have incorporated electronically communicated statements as conduct constituting stalking in anti-stalking laws. Some have both stalking and harassment statutes that criminalise threatening and unwanted electronic communications. Others have laws other than harassment or anti-stalking statutes that prohibit misuse of computer communications and email, or have passed laws containing broad language that can be interpreted to include cyberstalking behaviours.

Many of these laws fail to cover important forms of cyberstalking, including: when a perpetrator makes a threat to a victim by posting on a blog or a website instead of directly sending an email or message to the victim; when third parties harass the victim at the perpetrator's behest, or in the case of 'high-tech stalking', which involves the use of GPS devices, IP detectors and identity theft to harass victims.

Laws against cyberstalking are complicated by a number of other factors: that internet service providers and social media companies often do not cooperate in providing data crucial to proving a crime has been committed; that stalkers can delete messages and postings from their accounts; that the internet has no borders and that the stalking activity can be perpetrated on, or routed to, a server on the other side of the world.

Types of legal action

Victims have a number of legal means to take action against a stalker. Often the courts wish to assist, but stalking cases can be very complicated and convoluted and judicial decision-makers are ultimately constrained by the law and the sorts of remedies available to the court.

Criminal

Criminal prosecutions occur when police and prosecutors believe that a stalker has perpetrated a crime or crimes, such as acts of harassment, falsifying documents, damaging property or threats and/or acts of violence. Such offences are subject to criminal law standards of proof.

Civil: Restraining orders

The most widely used civil action against stalkers are restraining orders, also called intervention orders and anti-harassment injunctions. Such an order can be specific as to the actions forbidden (such as prohibiting the stalker to come within a certain distance of the victim) and duration, or it may be general and without a fixed time limit.

They do have disadvantages. To apply for an order against a stalker, a victim is usually advised to have legal representation, which can be expensive. If the stalker is intent on challenging the application, the order can be difficult to obtain and even more difficult to enforce. As lawyer Vic Rajah says, 'Intervention orders may become a battleground for the stalker.' Typically, a victim is forced to accept a mere undertaking, which a stalker can violate with near impunity. Violations are subject to arrest, at which point the matter becomes criminal.

Defamation

For the victim, one of the most confronting aspects of stalking is when the perpetrator uses others to do the harassment. This is known as stalking by proxy. As Vic Rajah says, 'Stalkers can gather others, even government and official bodies, to do their bidding for them.' They may send employers and work colleagues wild and exaggerated stories about the victim, as happened to Barbara (see pages 65–77), or make formal complaints to a professional body the victim belongs to. For the person who is on the wrong end of the stalker, this can be disorientating and debilitating, in part because the stalking may not be readily apparent. 'It can be sophisticated and it is very hard to stop by using legal means.' Thus this can perpetuate the culture of victim blaming.

A stalker spreading lies about a victim is guilty of defamation. But in many jurisdictions it is difficult to bring a successful defamation claim unless you can prove you have suffered economic loss. 'This is very difficult to quantify in the case of an individual because personal reputations are worth a very limited amount from an economic loss perspective,' Vic Rajah says. 'That means, taking a cost/benefit approach, it is hardly worthwhile launching a defamation case to recover a few hundred thousand dollars, even if the claim is deemed worthy of such a payout. If they do not meet the required burden of proof, victims may end up facing huge legal bills and also having costs awarded against them. Even if costs are awarded, the legal fees may outweigh any costs awarded and there is the real prospect that the stalker may not have sufficient financial means to satisfy a judgement made against them.

'In many ways defamation is a battle of wills, in the sense that if a person sues for defamation then they are issuing a challenge to the person who has defamed them to prove the truth of the statement made,' Vic Rajah says. 'But that opens up the victim's life to intense public scrutiny and in the end they may feel it would have been better not to have sued for defamation. In the right circumstances, though, it is a worthwhile action, but it is a tool of limited application and applies in some situations when people accept the risks and feel that they must recover their good reputation.'

Appendices

Appendix 1
Why Do They Do It?

Of all the work I've done in preparing this book, all the research and interviews, this is the moment I feared the most. I'm about to come face to face with a convicted perpetrator who was now free to walk the streets again. The fact that this is a person who targeted someone else, and is a complete stranger to me, doesn't make me feel much better. My own experience of being stalked, and everything I've learned about stalking, make me certain this is someone to be wary of – someone who is capable of obsessive, manipulative, unpredictable and dangerous behaviours. And yet, at the same time, I fully expected to be underwhelmed when I met him. I know from first-hand experience that stalkers aren't the bogeymen we see in our nightmares or in Hollywood films. They aren't necessarily shadowy characters hiding in alleyways. They can be clean-cut, well-presented, educated professionals who can appear to be perfectly 'normal' to the rest of the world. Indeed, this is a huge part of their power and the way they convince others to support them against their target. They sometimes have what is considered to be high public standing, are known as 'good citizens.' As I approached the meeting place, I felt my heart rate increase and I wrestled with the old emotions of fear and helplessness, which were so cleverly instilled in me by the perpetrator who had torn my own innocent world apart.

When I entered the room, James was sitting quietly dressed in a suit and tie. He was clean-cut and very welcoming. I examined him closely, looking for the signs – a twitch, a villainous glance, a bullying stare. Nothing. He shook my hand. I waited for my instincts to evoke terror. Nothing. If I had not known of his relentless three-year pursuit of a woman in her 40s who had three children, I would have immediately regarded him as pleasant, and engage in conversation with him just as I would anyone else. And as we talked, I became more aware of his disarmingly charming manner.

James had met Carly through a work colleague. He was from a stable family, had two sisters and one brother, and had grown up in a leafy, affluent suburb of a big city. To my knowledge he had no known prior stalking behaviour. He now works in the corporate sector and is in a senior management position with a multinational company, after having been found guilty and serving time in jail.

'So, James,' I said, 'why have you agreed to the interview?'

He replied calmly. 'Well, I guess I want you to understand what it's like, what they call stalking, what it's really like – what it feels like to me. I want to talk about it now because I am not hiding it any more. For years I spent a lot of my life either actively stalking Carly, being punished for stalking Carly or recovering from stalking Carly. When I was doing it, I thought about her all the time – what was she doing, where was she, who was she talking to, how I could get closer to her. I couldn't get the thoughts out of my head. I would wake up thinking about her and she was my last thought each and every night. I would write down plans to infiltrate her life. I used to have over 300 pictures of her on my computer and my phone. Sometimes I would sit outside her house and photograph her from across the road behind the big trees.

'I scanned Facebook and the internet and tried to befriend her friends. I would follow her schedule every day of the week. If she changed the schedule, I got stressed, very stressed. My job involved being out on the road visiting clients and I would make sure the visits coincided with watching Carly at some point each day. Sometimes she caught me watching her, sometimes she didn't.

'It started at a barbecue. She was very attractive and friendly and her personality was so bright. I had never met anyone like her before. She gave me a lot of attention and, after I offered to help financially with a charity she was involved in, she suggested we could catch up the next week for coffee. She was kind, smart and lived a completely different life to mine. She made it clear at the start that she had a partner, but I just didn't want to hear that. I didn't care. I wanted her. I had never experienced anything like the feeling I instantly had for her. I couldn't get enough of her and when she got scared off and stopped our catch-ups I didn't cope. I was depressed and I constantly thought about her and how I could get her. My thoughts scared me sometimes, but I kept up my job and my friendships. All the other parts of my life looked very normal.

'When the stalking increased and I started doing sneaky things to bully her into seeing me, I convinced people around me that Carly was the crazy one. I had a good reputation, so why wouldn't anyone believe me? I was popular and had been around for years – I guess I played off that a bit because people trusted me and I got a lot of them on side. I never stopped to think about her. I only thought of me – *and us.*

'I convinced one of my friends that Carly was a crazy, neurotic woman who wanted to hook up with me. He believed me and helped me hack into her computer – which allowed me to send these crazy emails to her work colleagues so they would think she was mad. I thought that if they sacked her, she would come running to me. I tried to make her feel vulnerable – well, as much as I could. In the early stages I told her that people were saying nasty things about her. Then, when she'd send me an upset text message in response, I'd show other people what she had sent me, not what I had said to her to provoke that reaction. I would then turn to Carly and be the hero. In her eyes I was defending her against wicked people spreading vicious rumours. She started to feel unbalanced. I could see it affected her.

'I would phone her over and over just to hear her voice. Then, when she changed numbers, I tricked one of her friends into giving me the new number. I continued calling her over and over again – sometimes 50 or 60 times a day, sometimes at night. I would get a fix when I heard her voice and then hang up.

'I could tell she was worn down, stressed and depressed. The more she weakened, the stronger I felt. When she sent her brother to my house to plead with me to stop, I got a high just knowing that my relentless advances were affecting her and she was noticing me. It was working.

'I never stopped.

'A lot of it was anonymous and whenever I did have direct contact with her I was always careful that there were no witnesses to hear my threats. I sent parcels to her door but they couldn't track them to me. I would spend hours working out my next move. I told mutual friends very convincing stories about her being crazy, neurotic and harassing me and that she was the culprit.

'Then I guess I went too far. I saw her talking to an older man one night, a stranger, outside her house. He left and she lingered with her little dog outside the front of her house. I knew her partner was out of town. I was already planning ways I would separate them but now there was this new guy. I went crazy because he wasn't in the plan. I was blinded by jealousy – *Why was she talking to him and not me? Who was he?* I ran out of the bushes and grabbed her, shaking her, threatening her, screaming at her. I was obsessed by her. She was driving me crazy. She broke away from me, ran inside and locked the door. I belted on the door. I could hear her kids screaming inside, but I couldn't stop. I don't even remember how long I was there. When the police arrived, it all sort of went downhill from there. Then they found the pictures of her and the computer stuff. I guess there was a lot they uncovered. It went bad for me and I ended up serving time.

'I hear she moved away,' James says. 'I don't know where. Just talking about it now is bringing it all back.'

He was more preoccupied about what it had done to his life. 'I guess I am still not totally over it,' he says. 'I don't know whether I can continue talking about it. Best I stop now.'

'So, James, if Carly walked into this room what would you do?'

He stared out of the window for what seemed like an eternity. Finally he said, 'I honestly don't know. But I know I haven't felt this way about anyone else in my life, or anyone I met before Carly. I wouldn't know until she was in front of me.'

I hoped that he never had contact with Carly again.

Appendix 2

The Incidence of Stalking Around the World

Rates of stalking, bullying and harassment are difficult to report for several reasons: 1) they are often not reported to police, 2) definitions are inconsistent, 3) data are often combined with domestic violence findings, and 4) data may be obtained from distinct groups, such as women or professional associations. In the European Union, for example, in 2017 21 states had laws against stalking but all '21 legal definitions differ from each another, and not just regarding the details'. The statistics given here are from official sources such as crime statistics, surveys of specific groups and, for European Union countries, a 2014 survey, *Violence Against Women: An EU-wide survey* (EU 2014), which was restricted to women's reported experiences of stalking.

The Istanbul Convention, which came into force on 1 August 2014, is the most far-reaching international treaty to tackle violence against women and domestic violence. Its comprehensive set of provisions spans far-ranging preventive and protective measures as well as a number of obligations to ensure an adequate criminal justice response to serious violations of human rights. The Convention sets up a monitoring mechanism to assess the level of implementation by its Parties.

Country	Stalking statistics	Legislation
Australia	One in every ten Australians experiences stalking victimisation, many suffering psychological, social or physical harm as a result; 66% move house to escape (Australia Bureau of Statistics).	**ACT:** *Crimes Amendment Act 2000, Crimes Act 1900,* s. 35 **NSW:** *Crimes (Domestic and Personal Violence) Act 2007* **NT:** *Domestic and Family Violence Act 2007,* s. 7 **QLD:** *Criminal Code Act 1899,* ss. 359A and 359B **SA:** *Criminal Law Consolidation Act 1935,* s. 19AA **TAS:** *Criminal Code Act 1924,* s. 192 **VIC:** *Crimes* Act *1958,* s. 21A **WA:** *Criminal Code Act Compilation Act 1913,* s. 338D
Austria	A small 2008 study found 11% incidence of stalking in Eastern Austria.	Stalking is defined as 'persistent persecution' in the *Criminal Code* s. 107a.

Belgium	24% of women experienced stalking since the age of 15 (EU, 2014).	*Criminal Code*, article 442bis covers stalking. Defined as 'The repeatedly pursuing, watching or harassing of a person in a way this person perceives to be disturbing, worrying or tormenting.'
Canada	In 2009, Canadian police reported just over 20,000 incidents of criminal harassment, almost 5% of all violent crimes reported to police. The rate of criminal harassment had been gradually increasing over the previous decade. Reports of criminal harassment to police increased by 7% from 2008 to 2009 (Canadian Centre for Justice Statistics).	*Criminal Code*, R.S.C. 1985, c. C–46, s. 264
Denmark	24% of women experienced stalking since the age of 15 (EU, 2014).	No criminalisation. Denmark had included the crime of stalking in its penal code since 1933; however, according to an EU report in 2017, Denmark does not currently have any laws criminalising stalking.
France	Nearly one in three French women have experienced harassment (EU, 2014).	222–33–2 *Criminal Code* against harassment.
Germany	Lifetime stalking prevalence of 15% – 19.4% for women & 11.4% for men (Hellman & Kliem, 2015).	*Protection Against Violence Act* 2002, and *Violence Protection Act* 2007.

Greece	12% of women experienced stalking since the age of 15 (EU, 2014).	No criminalisation.
Ireland, Republic of	12% of women experienced stalking since the age of 15 (EU, 2014). Incidents of recorded complaints rose from 97 in 2000 to 759 in 2008. A 2010 survey found that 25.1% of psychiatrists had been stalked at some time in their careers.	*Non-Fatal Offences Against the Person Act 1997*, s. 10 The Act does not use the term 'stalking'; the Minister for Justice at the time s. 10 was introduced commented that it was 'enacted in order to permit intervention to stop and punish conduct amounting to stalking at earlier stages than had been possible before then, and to obviate the need to rely on invocation of assault and criminal damage provisions.'
Italy	18% of women experienced stalking since the age of 15 (EU, 2014).	612bis *Criminal Code*, which came into force in 2009.
The Netherlands	26% of women experienced stalking since the age of 15 (EU, 2014).	Article 285b of the *Criminal Code*. The sentence can be up to three years of imprisonment, and a fine with a maximum of 11,250 euros.

New Zealand	No specific stalking data is captured by government statistics. A 2014 survey found that 87% of politicians reported experiencing harassment. A 2016 survey of women over 18 found that 52% had experienced online harassment; for those under 30, the figure was 72%	*Harassment Act 1997.*
Spain	11% of women experienced stalking since the age of 15 (EU, 2014).	172ter *Criminal Code,* came into force 2015.
Sweden	33% of women experienced stalking since the age of 15 (EU, 2014).	Chapter 4 §4b *Criminal Code,* came into force 2011, amended 2015.
Turkey		Stalking is recognised as a form of violence against women; implementation based on the Istanbul Convention (an international treaty on violence against women) – does not provide a definition or contain specific anti-stalking provisions.

| United Kingdom | Lifetime stalking prevalence of 15% – 20.2% of women & 9.8% of men (Office for National Statistics 2016).

Since ss. 111 and 112 were inserted into the Act, the number charged and reaching a first hearing has increased for the offences of:

• *stalking with fear/ alarm/distress* – from 72 people in 2012–13 to 643 in 2015–16

• *stalking involving fear of violence* – from 9 in 2012–13 to 128 in 2015–16

• *stalking involving serious alarm/ distress* – from 10 in 2012–13 to 331 in 2015–16

Scotland: In 2014–15, 1240 cases were commenced and 688 convicted. | **England & Wales:** *The Protection from Harassment Act 1997*, ss. 111 and 112.

Scotland: *Criminal Justice and Licensing (Scotland) Act 2010.* This was the first time stalking was recognised in legislation anywhere in the UK. The legislation sought to create a specific offence of stalking and a wider offence of threatening, alarming or distressing behaviour. |

| USA | According to US Bureau of Justice Statistics:

During a 12-month period an estimated 14 in every 1000 persons aged 18 or older were victims of stalking.

46% of victims felt fear of not knowing what would happen next.

Nearly 3 out of 4 victims knew their offender in some capacity.

More than half the victims lost 5 or more days from work because of the stalking.

A 2015 University of Alaska Anchorage survey of Alaskan women showed that more than a third had been stalked in their lifetime. | Federal law 18 U.S.C. § 2261A. |

Appendix 3

Resources

Australia

Aboriginal & Torres Strait Islander Women's Legal & Advocacy Service (Queensland) P: 1800 442 450 A: PO Box 5631, West End, 4101, QLD E: admin@atsiwlsnq.org.au W: www.atsiwlsnq.org.au	A community legal centre that provides free legal advice, information, assistance and referrals to support Aboriginal & Torres Strait Islander Women in Queensland.
Alopecia Resource Centre P: 0408 722380 A: 28–32 Gloucester Avenue Berwick, VIC W: www.alopeciacentre.com.au	Alopecia and hair loss is often linked to bullying episodes.
Anti Bullying Council Foundation E: info@antibullyingcouncil.org.au W: www.antibullyingcouncil.org.au	A not-for-profit organisation providing information and public awareness around the issues of bullying.

Brodie's Law W: www.brodieslaw.org	Victoria's anti-bullying legislation known as Brodie's Law commenced in 2011 and made serious bullying a crime punishable by up to 10 years' imprisonment. Sadly, Brodie Panlock aged 19 committed suicide after being systematically bullied at her place of work.
Bully Zero Foundation P: 03 9094 3718 W: www.bzaf.org.au	Provides cyber safety programs nationally for schools, workplaces, sporting clubs and community groups.
Bullying Fact Sheet W: www.adcq.qld.gov.au/ resources/brochures-and-guides/ fact-sheets/bullying-factsheet	Useful webpage from the Anti Discrimination Commission Queensland covering Queensland anti-bullying legislation.
Bullying No Way W: www.bullyingnoway.gov.au	A federal government website providing anti-bullying information and resources for students, parents and teachers.
Calley Rajah Law Firm Partner Vic Rajah P: 03 9781 4222	A caring law firm dealing with family law.
Community Legal Centres P: 02 9212 7333 W: www.naclc.org.au/cb_pages/ clcs.php (national organisation)	Independently operated not-for-profit, community-based organisations offering free legal and related services to the public. Located through metropolitan, regional, rural and remote locations. Check website for closest location.
Dolly's Dream W: www.antibullyingcrusader. com	The Dolly's Dream Foundation is established by family and friends of Dolly Everett. Dolly was a victim of bullying and ended her life at age 14.

eSafety Commissioner W: www.esafety.gov.au	Website of Office of eSafety Commissioner (established 2015) offers resources about online safety, including guides, training and education programs.
Head Space P: 1300 737 616 W: www.headspace.org.au	National youth mental health foundation dedicated to improving well-being of youth. Offers school workshops on bullying prevention.
Kids Helpline P: 1800 55 1800 W: www.kidshelpline.com.au	A free, private and confidential 24/7 phone and online counselling service for those aged 5 to 25. Partners with leading research organisations to develop more effective services.
Indigenous Women's Legal Line P: 1800 639 784 & 02 8745 6977 W: www.wlsnsw.org.au	Provides free and confidential legal information, advice and referrals for Aboriginal and Torres Strait Islander women in NSW; open Mon, Tue, Thurs 10am–12.30pm.

Legal Aid E: info@probonocentre.org.au W: www.probonocentre.org.au/legal-help/legal-aid/ Phone numbers for states & terrritories ACT: 1300 654 314 NSW: 1300 888 529 NT: 1800 019 343 QLD: 1300 651 188 SA: 1300 366 424 TAS: 1300 366 611 VIC: 1300 792 387 WA: 1300 650 579	In each state and territory, legal aid commissions provide assistance in criminal, family and civil law matters. The website of the Australian Probono Centre, located at the University of NSW, provides web links to your state or territory legal aid service.
Lifeline P: 13 11 14	24-hour hotline providing crisis support and suicide prevention services.
National Sexual Assault, Family and Domestic Violence Counselling Service P: 1800 RESPECT (1800 737 732)	24-hour national sexual assault, family and domestic violence counselling and support hotline for anyone who has experienced or is at risk of experiencing sexual assault, family and domestic violence.
Reflection Psychology Gary Rubin P: 03 9809 4888	Counselling for victims of stalking and bullying episodes.

Stop Stalking Now Foundation Ltd E: enquiry@ stopstalkingnowfoundation.org. au W: www. stopstalkingnowfoundation.org. au	Established to support victims through education and public awareness to address the issues of stalking and bullying.
Student Wellbeing Hub W: www.studentwellbeinghub. edu.au	Website resources to create learning communities that promote student wellbeing and the development of respectful relationships.
Suicide call back services P: 1300 659 467 W: www.suicidecallbackservice. org.au	A nationwide service that provides phone, video and online professional counselling to anyone contemplating or affected by suicide.
Victim Support Australia Phone numbers for states & territories victims support services: ACT: 1800 822 272 NSW: 1800 633 063 NT: 1800 672 242 QLD: 1300 139 703 SA: 1800 842 846 TAS: 1300 300 238 VIC: 1800 819 817 WA: 1800 818 988	Advances the interests of people victimised by crime. Helps victims, witnesses and their families and friends to manage the effects of crime and guide them through the legal process.

Women's Legal Services Australia W: www.wlsa.org.au	National network of community legal centres specialising in women's legal issues.

Canada

Canadian Centre for Occupational Health and Safety W: www.ccohs.ca/oshanswers/psychosocial/bullying.html	'Bullying in the Workplace' information, with advice about how to take action against it.
Canadian Red Cross W: www.redcross.ca/how-we-help/violence--bullying-and-abuse-prevention/educators/bullying-and-harassment-prevention	Provides violence, bullying and abuse prevention programs.
Canadian Resource Centre for Victims of Crime P: 1-877–232–2610 W: www.crcvc.ca	Provide free initial legal advice, support and information on stalking, bullying and harassment.
Fight Cyberstalking W: www.fightcyberstalking.org	An online resource site for cyberbullying victims. 'Fight Cyberstalking Toolkit' can be downloaded.

Legal Aid Phone numbers & websites for state organisations: AB: 1–866–845–3245, www.legalaid.ab.ca BC: 1–866–577–2525, www.lss.bc.ca MB: http://www.legalaid.mb.ca/ NB: 506–444–2776, www.legal-info-legale.nb.ca NL: 1–800–563–9911, www.legalaid.nl.ca/index.html NT: http://www.justice.gov.nt.ca/boards-agencies/legal-aid-commission/ NS: http://www.nslegalaid.ca/ NU: http://nulas.ca/en/ ON: 1–800–668–8258, www.legalaid.on.ca PE: 902–368–6043 (Charlottetown); 902–888–8219 (Summerside), www.princeedwardisland.ca/en/information/justice-and-public-safety/legal-aid QC: 1–800–842–2213, www.barreau.qc.ca SK: www.legalaid.sk.ca YT: 1–800–661–0408 ext 5210, legalaid.yk.ca	Independent, publicly funded non-profit corporation providing legal assistance for criminal and civil matters.

Stalking is a Crime W: www.gov.mb.ca/justice/ crown/victims/domestic/pubs/ stalkingweb.pdf	A booklet published by Manitoba government.

Republic of Ireland

Bully 4U W: www.bully4u.ie	Provides anti-bullying programs and services for schools.
CONNECT P: 1800 477 477 W: www.connectcounselling.ie	Phone counselling service for adults who experienced abuse in childhood; also available for partners and relatives.
Crime Victims Helpline P: 116006 W: www.crimevictimshelpline.ie/help	Offers support and advice for victims of crime.
Victim Support at Court P: 01 872 6785 W: www.vsac.ie	Free counselling and support for prosecution witnesses and their families at court.

New Zealand

Bullying Free NZ W: www.bullyingfree.nz/	For schools and their communities. The organisation is aimed at bullying prevention.
Community Law P: 0800 499 488 (toll free) W: http://communitylaw.org.nz/	Local community law centres can provide free initial legal advice and information on stalking, bullying and harassment.

Legal Aid Services	Legal aid is government funding to pay for legal help if you can't afford a lawyer. You can apply for help for criminal court proceedings, civil disputes, family disputes or if you're a victim of a violent offence and want to apply for a non-contact order.
General enquiries P: 0800 2 LEGAL AID (0800 253 425) W: www.justice.govt.nz/courts/going-to-court/legal-aid/ **Auckland** A: BX10660 North Shore City P: 09 488 5440 E: AKLCriminallegalaid@justice.govt.nz (criminal) E: AKLFamilylegalaid@justice.govt.nz (family) E: AKLCivillegalaid@justice.govt.nz (civil) **Wellington** A: SX10146 Wellington P: 0800 2 LEGAL AID (0800 253 425) E: WGNCriminallegalaid@justice.govt.nz (criminal) E: WGNFamilylegalaid@justice.govt.nz(family) E: WGNCivillegalaid@justice.govt.nz (civil) **Christchurch** A: DX WX11123, Christchurch 8443 P: 03 339 4730 E: christchurch.legalaid@justice.govt.nz	

Lifeline P: 09 522 2999 (Auckland) P: 0800 543 354 (outside Auckland) W: www.lifeline.org.nz	Lifeline's telephone counselling service provides 24 hour a day, 7 day a week counselling and support. Calls are confidential and free and you will speak to a trained Lifeline counsellor.
NetSafe P: 0508 NETSAFE (0508 638 723) – free helpline W: www.netsafe.org.nz	Information and advice about cyberbullying for young people, parents and teachers. Also offers text-based preventative advice and how-to guides.
New Zealand's Self-Help Legal Site W: www.howtolaw.co.nz	Find a lawyer. Includes self-help legal documents and 'how to' articles.
NZ Family Violence Clearinghouse W: library.nzfvc.org.nz	Library resource guide with articles on stalking.
Pink Shirt Day W: www.pinkshirtday.org.nz	New Zealanders stand together to take action against bullying.
Victim Support A: 180 Molesworth St Wellington, New Zealand P: 0800 victim (0800 842 846) E: nationaloffice@victimsupport.org.nz W: www.victimsupport.org.nz	This free service provides 24/7 emotional and practical support, information, referral to other support services and advocacy for the rights of victims.
Victims Information Service P: 0800 650 654: 24/7 helpline W: www.victimsinfo.govt.nz	Provides people affected by crime quick and easy access to information about their rights, support services and the criminal justice system.

United Kingdom

Action Against Stalking W: **www.actionagainststalking.org**	This website provides helpful information for anyone who is being stalked.
Anti-bullying Network E: info@antibullying.net W: www.antibullying.net	Website offering advice and an anti-bullying service that includes the provision of training, publications and consultancy services.
Beat Bullying E: info@beatbullying.org.uk W: www.beatbullying.org	Website offering articles, advice and resources to manage bullying and improve mental and emotional wellbeing.
Live Fear Free P: 0808 8010 800 E: info@livefearfreehelpline.wales	Free helpline offering advice on sexual violence and violence against women.
National Domestic Violence Helpline P: 0808 2000 247	Free 24-hour helpline.
National Stalking Clinic A: Camlet 1, North London Forensic Service, A: Chase Farm Hospital, The Ridgeway, Enfield P: 020 8702 6104 E: nationalstalkingclinic@nhs.net W: www.fixatedthreat.com/nationalstalkingclinic.php W: www.beh-mht.nhs.uk/	This specialist service provides assessment and treatment services for individuals who engage in stalking behaviour.

National Stalking Helpline P: 0808 802 0300 E: advice@stalkinghelpline.org W: www.stalkinghelpline.org	Practical advice and information to anyone who is currently or previously has been affected by harassment or stalking, or who wants to support friends and family members who are experiencing stalking.
Network for Surviving Stalking E: scaredofsomeone@gmail.com W: www.scaredofsomeone.org	Offering advice and information to people affected by stalking; enabling early recognition and the opportunity to seek help.
Network for Surviving Stalking P: 07501 752741 E: campaign@nss.org.uk W: www.scaredofsomeone.org	NSS's website has useful advice and knowledge. NSS also invites victims' stories and experiences so it can raise awareness and campaign for change.
Paladin: National Stalking Advocacy Service P: 020 3866 4107 E: info@paladinservice.co.uk W: www.paladinservice.co.uk	Provides advocacy to anyone at risk of serious harm from a stalker. Gives initial advice and a detailed assessment to anyone who calls the service and is affected by stalking.
Protection Against Stalking P: 0808 802 0300 E: pasofficehq@gmail.com W: www.protectionagainststalking.org	Provides support to victims, particularly those at high risk of harm and provides education about stalking, victim safety and improving management of stalkers. Offers National Stalking Helpline (see above)
RISE P: 0300 323 9985 W: www.riseuk.org.uk/	Provides a free helpline for those affected by abuse from ex-partners, giving practical support to help them rebuild safer lives.
Surviving Stalking W: www.survivingstalking.com	Tracey Morgan's Weblog with advice for stalking victims.

Suzy Lamplugh Trust P: 020 7091 0014 E: info@suzylamplugh.org W: www.suzylamplugh.org	This organisation campaigns for policy and legislative change, research, training and advice.
Victim Support P: 0845 30 30 900 W: www.victimsupport.org.uk	Helpline for anyone affected by crime.

United States of America

Legal Help USA E: customerservice@legal-help-usa.org W: www.legal-help-usa.org	Free information on legal issues; low-cost lawyers, attorneys & legal aid, downloadable legal forms; free legal links & resources.
The Message Relay Center E: MessageRelayCenter@msn.com	Acts as a mediator between parents when communication is either undesired or too dangerous to be conducted when domestic violence or stalking is involved.
National Center for Victims of Crime A: 2000 M Street, NW, Suite 480 Washington, DC 20036 P: 202-467-8700 P: (800) FYI-CALL (victim helpline) P: (800)211-7996 (TTY) E: gethelp@ncvc.org W: www.victimsofcrime.org	Advocates for stronger rights, protections, and services for crime victims; provides education, training for professionals; and offers current information on victims' issues.

National Coalition Against Domestic Violence A: One Broadway, Suite B210 Denver, CO 80203 P: 303-839-1852 W: www.ncadv.org	Offers safety plans, resources and cosmetic and reconstructive support, connecting survivors of domestic violence to free medical providers around the country to repair injuries inflicted by an abusive spouse or partner.
National Domestic Violence Hotline P: 1-800-799-SAFE (7233)	If your stalking situation has a domestic violence component, the NDV Hotline offers 24/7 free phone support and assistance or via the live chat service.
NOVA (National Organisation for Victim Assistance) A: 1757 Park Rd, NW, Washington, DC 20010. P: 800 879 6682 or 202 232 6682 W: www.trynova.org/	Free 24-hour hotline that provides information and referral for victims to resources in their own states.
Privacy Rights Clearinghouse W: www.privacyrights.org/ Harassment-and-Stalking	Free consumer guides, articles and tips for persons experiencing stalking and harassment.
Safe Horizon Hotline P: 1-800-621-HOPE (4673) W: www.safehorizon.org/get-help/ stalking/#signs-of-stalking/	24-hour hotline. Provides assistance, advocacy and support to victims of stalking in New York City.
San Diego County Stalking Strike Force P: (619) 515-8900	Provides assistance to San Diego stalking victims.

Stalking Resource Center P: (202) 467-8700 E: src@ncvc.org W: www.victimsofcrime.org/our-programs/stalking-resource-center	The centre provides training that is victim-centred, research informed, and practice based, technical assistance and an information clearinghouse. The website is a resource for practitioners and victims, including information about stalking statutes, a guide to online resources and practitioner profiles.
Victim Connect Helpline P: 855-4-VICTIM (855-484-2846) Online chat: chat.VictimConnect.org W: www.victimconnect.org/crime-resources/stalking/	Helpline operates 9.30am–6.30pm ET, Mon–Fri. Provides information and referrals for victims of all crime.

INTERNET SAFETY

Digital Trust W: www.digital-trust.org/	Helping victims of digital and cyber abuse.
Wired Safety W: www.wiredsafety.org	A volunteer-run organisation helping victims of cyber-harassment, providing one-on-one help, resources and extensive information, and education on internet and interactive technology safety, privacy and security issues.
Working to Halt Online Abuse (WHO@) W: www.haltabuse.org/	A volunteer organisation to fight online harassment through education of the general public and law enforcement, and empowerment of victims.

Further Reading

Books

Richard Gallagher, *I'll be Watching You*, Virgin Books, London, republished as paperback 2002.

Linden Gross, *To Have or To Harm*, Warner Books, New York, 1994; reissued as *Surviving a Stalker: Everything You Need to Know to Keep Yourself Safe*, Marlowe & Company, New York, 2000.

J Reid Meloy (ed), *The Psychology of Stalking: Clinical and Forensic Perspectives*, Academic Press, San Diego CA, 1998.

J Reid Meloy, Lorraine Sheridan & Jens Hoffman (eds), *Stalking, Threatening, and Attacking Public Figures: A Psychological and Behavioral Analysis*, Oxford University Press, New York, 2008.

Paul E Mullen, Michele Pathé & Rosemary Purcell, *Stalkers and Their Victims*, Cambridge University Press, Cambridge, 2000.

D Orion, *I Know You Really Love Me: A Psychiatrist's Journal of Erotomania, Stalking, and Obsessive Love*, Macmillan, New York, 1997.

E Ogilvie, *The Internet and Cyberstalking*, Australian Institute of Criminology, Sydney, 2000.

Michele Pathé, *Surviving Stalking*, Cambridge University Press, Cambridge, 2002.

Debra A Pinals, *Stalking: Psychiatric Perspectives and Practical Approaches*, Oxford University Press, New York, 2007.

Mike Procter, *How to Stop a Stalker*, Prometheus Books, New York, 2003.

Martha Stout, *The Sociopath Next Door*, Broadway Books, New York, 2005.

LEA Walker, *The Battered Woman Syndrome*, Springer, New York, 1984.

TK Logan, Jennifer Cole, Lisa Shannon & Robert Walker, *Partner Stalking: How Women Respond, Cope, and Survive*, Springer, New York, 2006.

Government reports

LA Greenfeld & MR Rand, *Violence by Intimates. Analysis of Data on Crimes by Current or Former Spouses, Boyfriends, and Girlfriends*, U.S. Department of Justice, Washington DC, 1998.

BS Fisher, FT Cullen & MG Turner, *The Sexual Victimization of College Women*, National Institute of Justice, Bureau of Justice Statistics, Washington DC, 2000.

Safety Net, *Technology, Safety, and Privacy Issues for Victims of Domestic Violence*, National Network to End Domestic Violence, Washington DC, 2004.

P Tjaden & N Thoennes, *Stalking in America: Findings from the National Violence Against Women Survey*, U.S. Department of Justice Washington DC, 1998.

EL Von Heussen-Countryman, 'The Stalking Problem, and the Need for Legislation in Britain: Report to Parliament and the Home Office', NASH, 1995.

LG Wang (ed), *Stalking and Domestic Violence*, Current issues series, Novinka Books, ebook, 2004.

Articles

MJ Allen, 'Look who's stalking: Seeking a solution to the problem of stalking', *Web Journal of Current Legal Issues* 4, 1996.

R Arvey and M Cavanaugh, 'Using surveys to assess the prevalence of sexual harassment: Some methodological problems', *Journal of Social Issues* 51, 1995, pp 39–52.

C Baird, N Bensko, P Bell, et al, 'Gender influence on perceptions of hostile environment sexual harassment', *Psychological Reports* 77, 1995, pp 79-82.

D Burles, 'A problem of privacy', *Solicitors Journal* 860, 1997.

T Bahm, 'Eliminating "cyber-confusion",' 2003, http://www.ncvc.org/src/main.aspx?.

MP Brewster, 'Power and control dynamics in prestalking and stalking situations', *Journal of Family Violence* 18, 2003, pp 207–17.

'Cell phone tech maintains privacy', *Wired News*, 19 January

2004, http://www.wired.com/news/wireless/.

'Overview on U.S. federal statutes or laws pertaining to cyberstalking', *Cyber-Stalking.net*, 2004, http://www.cyber-stalking.net/legal_usfederal.htm.

H Conway, 'Protection from Harassment Act 1997', *Family Law* 1998, pp 714–15.

R D'Ovidio & J Doyle, 'A study on cyberstalking: Understanding investigative hurdles', *FBI Law Enforcement Bulletin* 72(3), 2003, pp 10–17.

J Finn, 'A survey of online harassment at a university campus', *Journal of Interpersonal Violence* 19, 2004, pp 468–83.

J Finn & M Banach, 'Victimization online: The downside of seeking services for women on the internet', *Cyberpsychology and Behavior* 3, 2000, pp 776–85.

WJ Fremouw, D Westrup & J Pennypacker, 'Stalking on campus: The prevalence and strategies for coping with stalking', *Journal of Forensic Sciences* 42(4), 1997, pp 666–69.

B Givens, 'Public records on the internet: The privacy dilemma', 2002, http://www.cfp2002.0rg/proceedings/proceedings/givens.pdf.

TM Gregoire, 'Cyberstalking: Dangers on the information superhighway', 2004, http://www.ncvc.org/src/main.aspx?dbID=DB_Cyberstalking814.

S Gardner, 'Stalking', *Law Quarterly Review* 1998, pp 33–39.

T Gillett, S Eminson & F Hassanyeh, 'Primary and secondary erotomania: Clinical characteristics and follow-up', *Acta Psychiatrica Scandinavia* 82, 1990, pp 65–69.

Home Office (UK), Unpublished statistics regarding *The*

Protection from Harassment Act in 1997, London, 1999.

L Kidder, R Lafleur & C Wells, 'Recalling harassment, reconstructing experiences', *Journal of Social Issues* 51, 1995, pp 55–67.

A Kranz, 'Helpful or harmful? How innovative communication technology affects survivors of intimate violence', 2001, http://www.vaw.umn.edu/documents/5survivortech/5survivortech.html.

RK Lee, 'Romantic and electronic stalking in a college context', *William & Mary Journal of Women and the Law* 4(2), 1998, pp 373–409.

T Lawson-Cruttenden, 'Is there a law against stalking?' *New Law Journal* 1996, pp 418–19.

T Lawson-Cruttenden & B Hussain, 'Psychological assault and harassment', *New Law Journal* 1996, pp 1326–27.

T Lawson-Cruttenden & N Addison, 'Harassment and domestic violence', *Family Law* 1997, pp 429–31.

– 'Protection from Harassment Act', *New Law Journal* 1997, p 483.

S Lewis & J Lewis, 'Work, family and well-being. Can the law help?' *Legal and Criminological Psychology* 2, 1997, pp 155–67.

MG McGarth & E Casey, 'Forensic psychiatry and the internet: Practical perspectives on sexual predators and obsessional harassers in cyberspace', *Journal of the American Academy of Psychiatry and the Law* 30, 2002, pp 81–94.

A Medlin, 'Stalking to cyberstalking, a problem caused by the Internet', 2002, http://gsulaw.gsu.edu/lawand/papers/fa02/medlin.

K Orland, 'Stalker victims should check for GPS', 6 February 2003, http://www.cbsnews.com/stories/2003/02/06/tech/main539596.shtml.

Privacy Rights Clearinghouse, 'Wireless communications: Voice and data privacy', 2002, http://www.privacyrights.org/fs/fs2-wire.htm.

LE Rogers, A Castleton & SA Lloyd, S.A. (1996). 'Relational control and physical aggression in satisfying marital relationships', in DD Cahn & SA Lloyd (eds), *Family Violence from a Communication Perspective*, Sage, Thousand Oaks CA, 1996, pp 218–39.

C Southworth, 'Safety on the internet', Violence Against Women on the Internet Online Course (Module 5), May 2002, http://cyber.law.harvard.edu/vaw02/module5.html.

E Spence-Diehl, 'Stalking and technology: The double-edged sword', *Journal of Technology and Human Services* 22(1), 2003, pp 5–18.

BH Spitzberg & G Hoobler, 'Cyberstalking and the technologies of interpersonal terrorism', *New Media & Society* 4, 2002, pp 71–92.

Stalking Resource Center, 'Stalking technology outpaces state laws', *Stalking Resource Center Newsletter* 3(2), 2003, pp 1, 4–5.

A Samuels, 'Protection from Harassment Act 1997', *Solicitors Journal* 1997, pp 426–27.

L Sheridan, R Gillett & G Davies, 'Stalking: Seeking the victim's perspective', *Issues in Legal and Criminological Psychology* 30, 1999.

P Tain, 'Restraining orders: The focus of summary stalking cases', *Solicitors Journal* 1998, p 465.

D Thomas, 'Harassment and the right to protest', *Solicitors Journal* 1998, p 304.

Texas Council on Family Violence, 'Information confidentiality held by governmental bodies: Legal history of the domestic violence movement', 2003, http://www.tcfv.org/tcfv-content/policy.php?itemid=17.

US Department of Justice, 'Cyberstalking: A new challenge for law enforcement and industry', 1999, http://www.usdoj.gov/criminal/cybercrime/cyberstalking.htm

US Department of Justice, 'Stalking and domestic violence: Report to Congress', 2001, http://www.ncjrs.gov/pdffiles1/ojp/186157.pdf.

G Virgo, 'Offenses against the person: Do-it-yourself law reform', *Cambridge Law Journal* 1997, pp 251–53.

C Wells, 'Stalking: The criminal law response', *Criminal Law Review* 1997, pp 463–71.

M Wendland, 'Belleville man accused of electronic voyeurism', *Detroit Free Press*, 6 September 2001, http://www.freep.com/money/tech/spy6_20010906.htm

Working to Halt Online Abuse, 'Online harassment statistics', 2004, http://www.haltabuse.org/resources/stats/index.shtml.

Acknowledgements

You never know when a predator may strike. They walk among us, they try to look and act like us, they are sometimes considered upstanding citizens within the community but once they identify, select and focus on you it all changes. They are hunters, calculating, cold and ruthless and you are their prey. You are the human target and you are being stalked.

– Rachel Cassidy

A message of thanks from Rachel Cassidy

I've had a very fortunate life that has at times included meeting and getting to know some high-profile individuals. I almost didn't share the list of people below with you as at times I've been targeted through the perpetrators' motives of jealousy and envy but the people I've mentioned on this list are simply some of the many inspiring people I've met along the way. Often you will see them in the media and wonder what they are really like. Well, I can only give you my humble opinion after spending some time with them. Whether the people I have named are publicly known or they are my family members or a special friend who has stood by my side for many, many years they have all in some way, along the way touched my world and left an impression.

Former Prime Minister John Howard, thank you for the interview I did with you many years ago and for being so gracious every time we met, showing an interest in the worthy causes I supported.

Former Prime Minister Tony Abbott for an honest, very raw interview many years ago.

Hon Kim Wells MP, state member for Rowville: Kim, we have known each other for over 20 years – thank you for your ongoing friendship, it means a lot to me, and for supporting my events at Parliament House.

The Hon Luke Donnellan MP, Minister for Roads, Road Safety and Ports, state member for Narre Warren North: I have known you for 12 years, Luke, and you have never wavered in your support of me and of my work. I've appreciated our catch-ups, your phone calls and kind words of encouragement over the years.

The Hon Michael Sukkar MP: thank you for your generous support of the charities I've been involved with.

Former politician Brendan Nelson, who gives great attention to detail – we had memorable catch-ups years ago and I appreciated your good advice.

To my dear friend Mark Wilson, I am so proud of how far you have come. I am grateful for meeting that first day, for all the phone calls, catch-ups and chats we have had as we have travelled on this journey. And they say behind every good man is a good woman – and in your case your beautiful wife

AnneMarie walks side by side with you. What a loving couple and a fabulous team you are.

Kerri-Anne Kennerley, who welcomed me on to her television show, provided delicious desserts for me and shared my love of shoes.

Bert Newton, who was always gracious and engaging the many times I appeared on his television show, with his quick wit and dynamic energy. It was a pleasure to get to know him and his lovely wife Patti.

Jack Levi (Elliot Goblet), our friendship spans over 25 years – can't believe it's that long since your hat party, Jack.

The late Tony Greig for being so candid during my interview with him many years ago.

Ian Thorpe for having me on the *Undercover Angels* television program. What a blast, we had a great time.

The late Stan Zemanek for having me on *Beauty and the Beast*. That was a fun time we had and I still remember the vibrancy of Jeannie Little – her distinctive voice, crazy antics and genuine compassion for others.

Deborah Thomas, who is such a smart, articulate lady. Thanks Deborah for the support you gave me at one of my previous launches many years ago at Parliament House in Canberra.

To Diane Dunleavy, thank you for your support over the years with raising funds for worthy causes I have been involved with. You always gave an enormous amount of your time.

I would like to express my deepest gratitude to Debbie Chalmers, who I've worked with for over 20 years. You have stood by me when the times got really tough. People can always be there in the good times but the test of true friendship is when adversity strikes and I always felt you walking by my side throughout the most difficult of times. I knew you were there.

To my good friend Kate, you were the first person to encourage me to write a book and I've achieved that now. Thank you, Kate.

My GP and friend Penny Bennett. As well as being our family doctor, I am proud to say you are also a dear friend. You always have a huge smile, encouragement and an absolutely fabulous sense of humour. A bucket load of thank yous for all the years you have looked after my family.

To Paul Wheelton, AM, a very humble philanthropist who gives so much to the community. Paul has always welcomed me into his circle of friends.

To associate professor Troy McEwan, who has an abundance of passion for her very valuable work. Thank you for the extended support you have given me over the years writing this book.

Rachel Robinson and Mattia Bondanza from the highly successful PR firm Rocket Comms – thanks for always believing in me.

Phil Ruthven, AM, founder and director of IBISWorld, I value the caring and compassionate mentor you have been to me.

Eric Castillo, thank you for your work as a passionate advocate to raise funds for programs helping victims who have been bullied or stalked.

To Ted and Andrew Nisbet and his lovely wife Ellie, who are good friends, thank you for your support.

To Cr Tony Holland, a humble man who always stood by me and with whom I enjoy a deep friendship.

To David, who we consider a member of our family. You have been a constant supporter and have helped me in so many ways without hesitation, for which I am very grateful.

To lawyer Vic Rajah and former MP and business owner Tammy Lobato, two of the most courageous people I know, who have risen above enormous challenges in life to achieve great personal and professional happiness and success.

Thanks to the incredible legal eagles I have grown to know and love dearly, led by a man I greatly respect and admire who has always stood by me and been there when I really needed a friend: Lionel Appelboom from CIE Legal, Steven Troeth from Gadens Lawyers who never faltered in his belief and support of me, Robert Toth whom I've known for over 15 years from Marsh & Maher Richmond Bennison Lawyers, and Joanna Renkin (she lights up a room) from Lander & Rogers law firm.

To the ever-optimistic Antoinette Khalil (my surrogate sister) and her partner Joe, thanks for being there for well over 20 years and for all your kind words and our happy times. You are both an important part of my family.

To PR expert Jane Speechley, thank you for being a force to be reckoned with – Jane, you are a powerhouse of strength to me.

To my Michael for your protection and ever-lasting support.

To my beautiful boys, who have grown into decent, caring young men with whom I share a loving bond. I am very fortunate you are both in my life.

To my incredible friend, sister and buddy Caroline Pirie, you have always been there for me and you're still there over 20 years later. Love you, Caroline, and your beautiful family.

To Heather Chalmers, my second mum and who has

often said I'm her third daughter – your love, guidance and compassion all these years has meant the world to me.

To Mary Trewby, my friend and my editor, and a very gifted and articulate writer in her own right. I am indeed very fortunate to have such a talented person as a part of the team.

To lawyer Tony Carbone, a trusted friend who encouraged me to become involved in spreading the word about these issues and lobbied people around him to support me. Tony has always believed in me and gave me great strength.

To lawyer Ian McDonald from Simpsons Law – my dear friend who, although he has never experienced any issues himself, manages to have such compassion and understanding of what others have endured.

MP Danielle Green you certainly welcomed me into Parliament House where we enjoyed good conversation and a lot of laughs.

To Vicki Standish and Sally Browne, thank you for the absolutely incredible work you both do in the not-for-profit sector. I am in awe of how much you both give to others and so grateful for your loving friendship that you have both shown me.

To Associate Professor Rosemary Purcell, forensic psychologist. You are truly dedicated and passionate about the work you do in your chosen field. A sincere thank you for your generosity with the time you spent with me, which gave me an insight into the very important work you do.

To Lisa Hanrahan and Paul Dennett of Rockpool Publishing – thank you both for your vision and tenacity to produce books with real-life Australian stories that resonate and touch so many people within the community. These stories might not be told without publishers like Rockpool believing in them and getting behind authors like myself.

To Wendy Stapleton and partner Paul Norton, Nick Theodossi, Leonie Hemingway and Claudia Keech OAM, thanks for being loyal and trusted friends and for what you give back to the community.

To lawyer Matthew Latham of Jones Day: Matthew's genuine interest in helping those who are most vulnerable in the community is well known and respected. Matt has been very supportive of my work, even with his exceptionally busy schedule he has always taken the time to assist me where he can.

To Brock and Matilda Stanfield, two very special young people with wisdom beyond their years – it's such a pleasure to get to know them.

To Dr Bennett Sheridan, I am sure there are many people who are grateful there are doctors who care as much as you do – and I am one of them.

Rocco and Josie Rositano for all the times you helped me with your wise advice.

To Ann Sweeney, a dear friend, and David Mann and John Mann, two really good men.

To Angela Carrettin and her wonderful family and my special friend Simone Kearney.

To Brien and Kathy Hansen – thanks Kathy for your support at my dad's funeral – Danielle and John, lawyer Bianca Salmon and Sandra – the sensational six. What a bunch of fabulous friends.

To Jade Raykovski for your tenacity with happily jumping in to help when needed.

Victorian police officer and friend Leeanne Trustler, who

has supported so many victims in a compassionate and humane way – which is a credit to her.

My sweet, kind and generous friend actor Tony Bonner AM.

To all my aunties, uncles and cousins out there – there are too many to name (we have a *big* family) – thanks for being a part of my journey of life.

To Gary Rubin, who is one of my trusted friends and has encouraged and rallied behind me to continue my work in the not-for-profit sector and to finish writing this book. Gary has considerable talent himself and, despite having a very full life, he continues to always make room for friends like myself. He is always there with an ear to listen and sound advice to give.

A big thank you to psychologist Lorraine Sheridan for her extended support with this book and to lawyer Mary Boardman, a passionate advocate supporting victims of bullying and stalking no matter where they live in the world.

To the many victims who appear in this book and those I spoke to whose stories are not included but who bravely shared their experiences with me, a huge thank you. Victims who repeated stories over and over of how perpetrators would seek to control their lives, sometimes making wild accusations and/ or using government or legal avenues that meant the victim had to constantly defend themselves as they were placed under a microscope. They sometimes endured physical threats and at times threats to family and friends. Their lives were constantly disrupted, leading to careers ruined, relationships lost and health compromised. A well-respected Australian personality once said to me, 'Rachel, bullies and their supporters can collectively be so conniving and manipulative that they could even make Mother Teresa look guilty'. The courage it takes to stand tall after being attacked in such ways is considerable, so my deepest gratitude to all those who stepped forward to make a difference and show support for other victims.

To all the experts who freely gave their time and energy to me as I was researching this book and were so open and generous during my interviews with them. They are clearly very passionate and dedicated to the work they do in their respective fields.

To all the other supporters, and my wonderful circle of family and friends, there are many of you, and you know who you are. I am truly grateful to each one of you for standing by me and for playing your role in being a part of my life.

A message of thanks and acknowledgements from Mark Wilson

To my dear friend Rachel Cassidy, who sat with me in a coffee shop where we both poured our hearts out having only just met. Together we felt the need to share, to do something about the injustice and challenge the world to share the burden of victims of stalking, their friends and families.

To the many dancers in our studios who showed loyalty and support and shouldered the burden of the fires. You can burn a studio down but you can't take away the dancer within. Dance on dancers!

The Victoria Police who searched high and low for the perpetrators and have left the case open. In particular, Dave Bruce who will always be a friend.

To my good friend Dr Bill Atkin, who helped me understand more about myself as both events happened. We no longer see each other, but you'll always be a close, dear friend.

To Channel 7 which paid for the hire of the Moonee Valley Function Centre where we held a fundraiser to pay for the loss of competitors' clothing and keep the studio running.

To dear, dear Todd McKenney, who gave of his time to sing (against doctor's orders), paid for a pianist and a singer to accompany him. It's the Todd most people don't know that I value most deeply.

To Daryl Somers, who paid for a band, gave his time freely and provided raffle prizes to keep us going. A kind and loving person who has given so much to Australian television and took time to give to us.

To the Yarra Plenty Church, now Planet Shaker, and in particular Richard White who sat having coffee with me so many times and would call just to say hi. You prayed for us and helped us through a tough time. God has worked through you to bring us out stronger. Bless you!

To our close friends, particularly the Kemp family, who fed us on many occasions when I couldn't provide for my family. It's a sobering feeling to not provide for your family and an uplifting feeling to be cradled by friends without judgement, just support. My love always.

To my brothers-in-law Michael, Geoffrey and Chris, who showed their strength and support in a crisis. Our loss was also your loss. We started this together and we all felt the pain.

To my mother-in-law Darlene Ryan, who passed away in recent years and was the loyal, passionate supporter throughout my whole career. I miss you and thank you for the great love of my life – Annemarie, my wife.

Thank you also to my father-in-law John Ryan, who has

always been there for me. Strong, wise, measured and focused. An important man in my life.

To my brothers Ian and Alan, who through the years have held my hand when I was not strong enough to stand on my own. I thank you both and will always love you. Your support has allowed me to take the steps on a new road.

To my mum Mary and dad Alan. You always taught me not to feel sorry for myself but stand strong and be the best I can be. Thanks to you instilling in me the love of God and faith in the future, I have a strong belief in the intrinsic goodness of humankind. Every day I try to look for the good in others without judging them. It's through your teachings I've learned to forgive and grow.

To my three children, who have had to bear having a stalker in our lives and the losses forced on our family: the loss of the fun place you danced and played, the stress you had to witness that would not have been there otherwise. There have been great things you've learned also. To be strong, never let other people's actions stop you from being who you are as a gift to the world and to your mother and me. Believe in yourselves and know that a step back is a chance to rest and gather energy as you step forward again into a life of unlimited possibilities.

When you say, 'I do' at your wedding and commit to be together in good and bad times, no one expects they're saying yes to a stalker coming into your life because you are married to someone. Annemarie, the most wonderful person I know, has always struggled to understand all of this and she did not deserve what happened – but stayed with me anyway. So many times, you could have left. Our love is bigger than the actions thrust upon us. I love you and always will and thank you from the depths of my heart for always being with me. It matters when you say good luck, even when you think I don't need it. It really matters.

To the stalker, I forgive you and pray for your world. May you find peace and know that you're not hated for your actions. Try to grow and love the people around you as much as you can within your capabilities. If it helps, seek some support from the people around you if you feel the urge to act this way again. You have a society that's here to help.

To God, I don't understand all of this but know you have a bigger picture for the world that's beyond me. I love you father and thank you for being with me providing strength when human frailty existed. Please father, cradle the victims and forgive the perpetrators. Provide peace for all and help them love each other as you love us!